W9-AWI-965

AMY TAN

WOMEN of ACHIEVEMENT

AMY TAN

Charles J. Shields

CHELSEA HOUSE PUBLISHERS
PHILADELPHIA

Chelsea House Publishers
Editor in Chief Sally Cheney
Director of Production Kim Shinners
Production Manager Pamela Loos
Art Director Sara Davis
Editor Benjamin Kim
Production Editor Diann Grasse
Layout 21st Century Publishing and Communications, Inc.

The Chelsea House World Wide Web address is
http://www.chelseahouse.com

First Printing
1 3 5 7 9 8 6 4 2

Library of Congress Cataloging-in-Publication Data

Shields, Charles J., 1951–
    Amy Tan / Chip Shields.
        p. cm. — (Women of achievement)
    Includes bibliographical references (p.   ).
    Summary: Explores the life and career of Amy Tan, from her childhood in California, through her struggle to accept her Chinese heritage, to her career as a writer.
    ISBN 0-7910-5889-1 (alk. paper) — ISBN 0-7910-5890-5 (pbk. : alk. paper)
    1. Tan, Amy—Juvenile literature. 2. Novelists, American—20th century—Biography—Juvenile literature. 3. Chinese Americans—Biography—Juvenile literature. [1. Tan, Amy. 2. Authors, American. 3. Women—Biography. 4. Chinese Americans—Biography.] I. Title. II. Series.

PS3570.A48 Z88 2001
813'.54—dc21
[B]   2001047334

CONTENTS

WOMEN of ACHIEVEMENT

Jane Addams
SOCIAL WORKER

Madeleine Albright
STATESWOMAN

Marian Anderson
SINGER

Susan B. Anthony
WOMAN SUFFRAGIST

Joan of Arc
FRENCH SAINT AND HEROINE

Clara Barton
AMERICAN RED CROSS FOUNDER

Rachel Carson
BIOLOGIST AND AUTHOR

Cher
SINGER AND ACTRESS

Cleopatra
QUEEN OF EGYPT

Hillary Rodham Clinton
FIRST LADY AND ATTORNEY

Katie Couric
JOURNALIST

Diana, Princess of Wales
HUMANITARIAN

Emily Dickinson
POET

Elizabeth Dole
POLITICIAN

Amelia Earhart
AVIATOR

Gloria Estefan
SINGER

Jodie Foster
ACTRESS AND DIRECTOR

Ruth Bader Ginsburg
SUPREME COURT JUSTICE

Katherine Graham
PUBLISHER

Helen Hayes
ACTRESS

Mahalia Jackson
GOSPEL SINGER

Helen Keller
HUMANITARIAN

**Ann Landers/
Abigail Van Buren**
COLUMNISTS

Barbara McClintock
BIOLOGIST

Margaret Mead
ANTHROPOLOGIST

Julia Morgan
ARCHITECT

Toni Morrison
AUTHOR

Grandma Moses
PAINTER

Lucretia Mott
WOMAN SUFFRAGIST

Sandra Day O'Connor
SUPREME COURT JUSTICE

Rosie O'Donnell
ENTERTAINER AND COMEDIAN

Georgia O'Keeffe
PAINTER

Eleanor Roosevelt
DIPLOMAT AND HUMANITARIAN

Wilma Rudolph
CHAMPION ATHLETE

Diane Sawyer
JOURNALIST

Elizabeth Cady Stanton
WOMAN SUFFRAGIST

Martha Stewart
ENTREPRENEUR

Harriet Beecher Stowe
AUTHOR AND ABOLITIONIST

Barbra Streisand
ENTERTAINER

Amy Tan
AUTHOR

Elizabeth Taylor
ACTRESS AND ACTIVIST

Mother Teresa
HUMANITARIAN AND
RELIGIOUS LEADER

Barbara Walters
JOURNALIST

Edith Wharton
AUTHOR

Phillis Wheatley
POET

Oprah Winfrey
ENTERTAINER

"REMEMBER THE LADIES"

MATINA S. HORNER

"Remember the Ladies." That is what Abigail Adams wrote to her husband John, then a delegate to the Continental Congress, as the Founding Fathers met in Philadelphia to form a new nation in March of 1776. "Be more generous and favorable to them than your ancestors. Do not put such unlimited power in the hands of the Husbands. If particular care and attention is not paid to the Ladies," Abigail Adams warned, "we are determined to foment a Rebellion, and will not hold ourselves bound by any Laws in which we have no voice, or Representation."

The words of Abigail Adams, one of the earliest American advocates of women's rights, were prophetic. Because when we have not "remembered the ladies," they have, by their words and deeds, reminded us so forcefully of the omission that we cannot fail to remember them. For the history of American women is as interesting and varied as the history of our nation as a whole. American women have played an integral part in founding, settling, and building our country. Some we remember as remarkable women who—against great odds—achieved distinction in the public arena: Anne Hutchinson, who in the 17th century became a charismatic religious leader; Phillis Wheatley, an 18th-century black slave who became a poet; Susan B. Anthony, whose name is synonymous with the 19th-century women's rights movement, and who led the struggle to enfranchise women; and in the 20th century, Amelia Earhart, the first woman to cross the Atlantic Ocean by air.

These extraordinary women certainly merit our admiration, but other women, "common women," many of them all but forgotten, should also be recognized for their contributions to American thought and culture. Women have been community builders; they have founded schools and formed voluntary associations to help those in need; they have assumed the major responsibility for rearing children, passing on from one generation to the next the values that keep a culture alive. These and innumerable other contributions, once ignored, are now being recognized by scholars, students, and the public. It is exciting and gratifying that a part of our history that was hardly acknowledged a few generations ago is now being studied and brought to light.

In recent decades, the field of women's history has grown from obscurity to a politically controversial splinter movement to academic respectability, in many cases mainstreamed into such traditional disciplines as history, economics, and psychology. Scholars of women, both female and male, have organized research centers at such prestigious institutions as Wellesley College, Stanford University, and the University of California. Other notable centers for women's studies are the Center for the American Woman and Politics at the Eagleton Institute of Politics at Rutgers University; the Henry A. Murray Research Center for the Study of Lives, at Radcliffe College; and the Women's Research and Education Institute, the research arm of the Congressional Caucus on Women's Issues. Other scholars and public figures have established archives and libraries, such as the Schlesinger Library on the History of Women in America, at Radcliffe College, and the Sophia Smith Collection, at Smith College, to collect and preserve the written and tangible legacies of women.

From the initial donation of the Women's Rights Collection in 1943, the Schlesinger Library grew to encompass vast collections documenting the manifold accomplishments of American women. Simultaneously, the women's movement in general and the academic discipline of women's studies in particular also began with a narrow definition and gradually expanded their mandate. Early causes, such as woman suffrage and social reform, abolition, and organized labor were joined by newer concerns, such as the history of women in business and the professions and in politics and government; the study of the family; and social issues such as health policy and education.

Women, as historian Arthur M. Schlesinger, jr., once pointed out, "have constituted the most spectacular casualty of traditional history. They have made up at least half the human race, but you could never tell that by looking at the books historians write." The new breed of historians is remedying that omission. They have written books about immigrant women and about working-class women who struggled for survival in cities and about black women who met the challenges of life in rural areas. They are telling the stories of women who, despite the barriers of tradition and economics, became lawyers and doctors and public figures.

The women's studies movement has also led scholars to question traditional interpretations of their respective disciplines. For example, the study of war has traditionally been an exercise in military and political analysis, an examination of strategies planned and executed by men. But scholars of women's history have pointed out that wars have also been periods of tremendous change and even opportunity for women, because the very absence of men on the home front enabled them to expand their educational, economic, and professional activities and to assume leadership in their homes.

The early scholars of women's history showed a unique brand of courage in choosing to investigate new subjects and take new approaches to old ones. Often, like their subjects, they endured criticism and even ostracism by their academic colleagues. But their efforts have unquestionably been worthwhile, because with the publication of each new study and book another piece of the historical patchwork is sewn into place, revealing an increasingly comprehensive picture of the role of women in our rich and varied history.

Such books on groups of women are essential, but books that focus on the lives of individuals are equally indispensable. Biographies can be inspirational, offering their readers the example of people with vision who have looked outside themselves for their goals and have often struggled against great obstacles to achieve them. Marian Anderson, for instance, had to overcome racial bigotry in order to perfect her art and perform as a concert singer. Isadora Duncan defied the rules of classical dance to find true artistic freedom. Jane Addams had to break down society's notions of the proper role for women in order to create new social situations, notably the settlement house. All of these women had to come to terms both with themselves and with the world in which they lived. Only then could they move ahead as pioneers in their chosen callings.

Biography can inspire not only by adulation but also by realism. It helps us to see not only the qualities in others that we hope to emulate, but also, perhaps, the weaknesses that made them "human." By helping us identify with the subject on a more personal level they help us feel that we, too, can achieve such goals. We read about Eleanor Roosevelt, for instance, who occupied a unique and seemingly enviable position as the wife of the president. Yet we can sympathize with her inner dilemma; an inherently shy woman, she had to force herself to live a most public life in order to use her position to benefit others. We may not be able to imagine ourselves having the immense poetic talent of Emily Dickinson, but from her story we can understand the challenges faced by a creative woman who was expected to fulfill many family responsibilities. And though few of us will ever reach the level of athletic accomplishment displayed by Wilma Rudolph or Babe Zaharias, we can still appreciate their spirit, their overwhelming will to excel.

A biography is a multifaceted lens. It is first of all a magnification, the intimate examination of one particular life. But at the same time, it is a wide-angle lens, informing us about the world in which the subject lived. We come away from reading about one life knowing more about the social, political, and economic fabric of the time. It is for this reason, perhaps, that the great New England essayist Ralph Waldo Emerson wrote in 1841, "There is properly no history: only biography." And it is also why biography, and particularly women's biography, will continue to fascinate writers and readers alike.

Amy Tan was born to Chinese-immigrant parents in 1952. Her novel The Joy Luck Club *reflects the strained relations between immigrant parents and their teenage children—specifically, the relations between mothers and daughters.*

1

THE HYPHENATED AMERICAN

"You want me to be someone I'm not!" I sobbed. "I'll never be the kind of daughter you want me to be!"

"Only two kinds of daughters," she shouted in Chinese. "Those who are obedient and those who follow their own mind! Only one kind of daughter can live in this house. Obedient daughter!"

—from *The Joy Luck Club*

This scene from the acclaimed 1989 novel *The Joy Luck Club* by Amy Tan could have easily come from its author's own past. The stories in *The Joy Luck Club* of strained relationships between Chinese mothers and their Americanized daughters reflected the troubled bond that existed between Amy and her own mother, Daisy Tan, especially during Amy's teenage years.

Said Tan, "If you were to say to me when I was 17, 'You know, one day you're going to write a book about Chinese people and about your relationship with your mother and how much you love your mother,' and all this stuff, I would have said 'You are crazy. You are absolutely crazy. There is no way I would ever do that. . . . I'm never going to get along with my parents, never going to feel accepted by the other kids, never going to make it because I'm going to be held back with this enormous burden of—something or other—pressure, not being good enough.'"

It was not until Amy Tan was in her mid-thirties that she turned to writing the fiction in which she expressed herself, basing her first novel on the relationships of four Chinese immigrant mothers and their four American-born daughters. One critic praised *The Joy Luck Club* for its realistic portrayals: "Intensely poetic, startlingly imaginative and moving, this remarkable book will speak to many women, mothers and grown daughters, about the persistent tensions and powerful bonds between generations and cultures." Within weeks of its publication, *The Joy Luck Club* became an international best-seller, and ensured Amy Tan a place among America's best-known authors.

The girl who would become acclaimed for her skill as a writer was born to John and Daisy Tan (their Americanized names) on February 19, 1952. Amy's Chinese name was An-Mei, meaning "blessing from America." She was the middle child. The Tans already had a son, Peter, born in 1950. Another son, named John after his father, was born two years after Amy in 1954.

John and Daisy Tan had backgrounds that were not unusual for many Chinese-Americans who grew up in early 20th century China and came to the United States. However, their personal histories and family legends that emerged from storytelling about their pasts would provide Amy with many of the characters, incidents, heartbreaks, tragedies, and acts of courage that would become the cornerstones of her stories and novels.

John was an electrical engineer and Baptist minister who immigrated to America in 1947 to escape the turmoil of the Chinese Civil War. During that time, the Red Army of Chinese Communist revolutionary Mao Tse-tung was gradually sweeping the old pro-Western regime out of power, and it was widely known that friends of the former government would be considered enemies of the new Communist state. John, who worked for the United States Information Service after World War II ended in 1945, saw the handwriting on the wall and fled, as did thousands of other highly educated Chinese.

The story of why Daisy Tan was forced to leave China was infinitely sadder. In China, she had divorced an abusive husband, but lost custody of her three daughters, a source of grief she hid from her American daughter until Amy was an adult. She boarded the last ship sailing from the city of Shanghai for the West shortly before the Communist takeover in 1949, leaving behind her children, she believed, forever. Not long after her arrival in the United States, Daisy and John met and married, and settled in Oakland, California.

But to Amy, who had never known anything except life in the United States, her parents' past, and their awkward attempts to be newly minted Americans, caused unending pain and embarrassment. Amy was part of a new generation of Chinese-Americans who wanted to distance themselves from China. They considered themselves Americans, but faced difficulties.

New York Times book critic Orville Schell explained the difficulties faced by the children of Asian emigrants: "Unlike the children of European emigrants, they had obviously Oriental features, which made it difficult for them to lose themselves in the American melting pot. Living in the confinement of Chinatowns with parents who spoke broken

Amy's parents, Daisy and John Tan, immigrated to America from China to escape the Chinese Civil War. These refugees wave goodbye from the stern of the Castel Bianca *as they leave the Chinese port of Shanghai on December 31, 1948.*

English ('tear and wear on car,' 'college drop-off') and who clung to the old Chinese way, they felt an indelible sense of otherness that weighed heavily on them as they tried to make their way into middle-class American life."

Tan remembers that as a child she felt like an American girl trapped in a Chinese body. She once described how she tried to change the shape of her nose by pinching it with a clothespin, hoping it to make it narrower, less Asian. "There was shame and self-hate," she said when explaining her childhood efforts to understand where she truly belonged. "There is this myth that America is a melting pot, but what happens in assimilation is that we end up deliberately choosing the American things—hot dogs and apple pie—and ignoring the Chinese offerings."

"Chinese offerings," however—whether it was food, culture, appearance, or language—were things that Amy desperately wanted removed from her life. She recalls being ashamed when people came over to her house and saw that her mother was preparing food using fresh vegetables and serving fish with the head still on. Unlike her friends' mothers, Amy's mother didn't make TV dinners or use canned foods. This difference worried the young girl, who feared her friends would think that her parents were too poor to afford the more usual American fare.

When accompanying her mother in public, Amy squirmed with embarrassment. Daisy Tan wore uncoordinated outfits and mispronounced words in her Shanghai accent, which Amy's classmates loved to ridicule. Tan would later recall that as a child, and later a teenager, there was nothing the least bit amusing about being what she called "a hyphenated person," a Chinese-American.

Added to the psychological pressure of not wanting to be different, from the time she was about eight years old, Amy fought with her mother almost every day. The twin issues were success and obedience.

Having sacrificed so much to give their children a fresh start in a new country, the Tans naturally had high hopes for their children. They had fled from a country that was in many aspects as repressive and impoverished as it had been 1,000 years ago. Mrs. Tan in particular had suffered in ways still unknown to her daughter. Being among the lucky few who had arrived safely in the United States, the Tans, and other Chinese-Americans of their generation, found it incomprehensible that their children might not want the advantages that would have been denied to them in China.

Amy, on the other hand, found her iron-willed mother's constant emphasis on success unreasonable, hurtful, and almost unbearable. In an online interview with the Academy of Achievement, she recalled one incident that occurred early on in school, where she suffered over not meeting her parents' high expectations: "I was in kindergarten and there was a little girl who I didn't think was a very good artist," she remembered. "I thought I did a very careful [drawing of a] house, you know, with the chimney, and the windows, and the trees, and she was more of an abstract artist. Hers was very loose, and I didn't think it was very good but they decided to pin hers up in the Principal's office. So that was like getting the 'A.' My mother wanted to know, Why wasn't my picture in that window?"

Tan said she came to believe that achievement guaranteed approval, which in turn would bring the acceptance she craved. "I thought achievement had to do with gaining approval from other people—my parents, my teachers, then higher-ups," she said. "It was a plateau at one level and then a continual climbing, always seeking higher and higher levels of approval. That was what achievement was: the plateaus you always had to maintain, the highest standards, the 'A's.' People would give you the feedback and tell you if you had done the achievement." Tan even interpreted her parents' moves from 41st to 51st to 61st Street and Highland Avenue in Oakland as a demonstration that moving up in the world was essential.

But Amy's fears of not achieving success and

Amy's mother, Daisy (left), placed a constant emphasis on success. Amy admits to fighting with her mother almost every day from the time she was eight years old. The fights were usually over success and obedience.

gaining approval were small compared to the fear she had that her mother had total power over her—even the power of life and death. She recalled attending the funeral of one of her classmates who had died of leukemia. When her mother took her up to the casket, Amy remembers being terrified: "I saw Rachel's hands clasped over her chest, and her face was bloodless, and her hands were flat, and

I was scared, because this was the little girl I used to play with. My mother leaned over to me and she said, 'This is what happens when you don't listen to your mother.'"

As an adult Tan later realized that her mother was probably talking about her belief that the child had died because she hadn't washed pesticides off fruit before eating it, as parents will remind children to do. Perhaps Daisy Tan believed these toxic chemicals had caused the child's illness. Regardless, even if Amy misinterpreted the point, Mrs. Tan saw nothing wrong with injecting fear into children about the consequences of disobedience. Amy notes that her mother had been raised in an atmosphere of fear herself, and she strongly believed that fear was the way to control children for their own good.

As she grew up, it didn't seem to Amy that she would ever be out from under her mother's thumb, either—Mrs. Tan's control was that complete. Amy Tan would later recall that her parents put a great deal of pressure on her to be what they thought she should be when she grew up (a doctor) and in her spare time (a concert pianist). She herself had dreams of becoming an artist, although she realized that she wouldn't make much money being an artist. Yet as a young girl she remained anxious over whether she could ever fulfill the high expectations of her parents.

But then, to Amy's own amazement, and her parents' delight, she suddenly excelled at something competitive in the public arena—an event so transforming that it would inspire her to try her hand at fiction writing 25 years later. The local library in Santa Rosa, California, was holding an essay contest for elementary school students on the topic, "What the Library Means to Me." The winner would have his or her entry printed in the *Press Democrat* newspaper.

Tan recalled how she wrote her essay in the style of her minister father delivering a sermon:

> I tried to be very sincere, sort of go for the emotion, you know, about how the library is a friend. And this really all was very sincere, but at the end (this is why I think I won this essay contest), I made a pitch for money, which, of course, is what ministers do at the end of their talks. And I said how I had given (I think it was) 17 cents, which was my entire life savings at age eight, to the Citizens for Santa Rosa Library, and that I hoped that others would do the same.

She won. Not only did her essay appear in print in the local newspaper, but she also won a transistor radio—the ultimate symbol of being an American teenager, of belonging to the "in crowd" during the rock 'n' roll era of the 1950s. And "at that moment," she recalled, "there was a little gleam in [my] mind that maybe writing could be lucrative."

Almost unknown to Amy, in fact, as she was growing up, the art of storytelling was seeping into her, although the subjects were not ones she would have thought anyone would have cared about. Her father influenced her a great deal. Constantly busy with his duties as a minister, he combined work and family time by practicing his sermons aloud in front of his daughter to see what Amy thought of them and determine whether there were parts she didn't understand. She would remember how the sermons seemed like stories, and that she very much enjoyed hearing them.

And Amy could not avoid being influenced by her mother, often hearing Daisy Tan's endless stream of stories, as well, during her childhood. Tales involving superstitious events, promises made and broken, marriages and deaths, and families coming together and falling apart ran for years in the background of the Tans' home. Amy recalls, "There was a lot of storytelling going on in our house: family stories, gossip, what happened to the people left behind in China. The gossip about people's character that went around as my aunt and my mother shelled peas on the dining table covered with newspaper."

Listening to the comfortable murmur of Shanghainese and Mandarin words, Amy found herself being drawn by the mysterious power of words. Although she stopped speaking Chinese when she was five, she remained very interested in the power of words: "Words to me were magic. You could say a word and it could conjure up all kinds of images or feelings or a chilly sensation or whatever. It was amazing to me that words had this power."

Sometimes Amy could not resist interrupting her mother to ask a question, which would lead to a whole new round of storytelling—events linked to one another by a single remark or glance between people long ago, a distinctive sound, or even a remembered aroma: "I'd ask a simple question. I'd say, 'Oh, did you have good vegetables in that part of China?' She'd say, 'Oh, well, yes, but then once when I was gathering mushrooms. . . . Oh that time, the mushrooms, that man died, but then that was his fault, because, you know. . . .' And then she'd just lead into something else. I'd say, 'I asked a simple question!'"

But if her mother's stories sometimes seemed long-winded, rambling, or tiresome, Amy discovered there was another place, a private one, where she could still enjoy stories and words of her own choosing—in books. Reading became a refuge where she could escape from her stressful home life, which too often overflowed with her anxiety and her tensions with her mother. Because Amy so enjoyed escaping the pressures of her world in reading, she actually feared that her parents would think it was wrong and try to take the books away.

Although the Tan home didn't contain many books—outside of the Bible, a medical textbook, a set of encyclopedias, and *Readers Digest* condensed books—Amy managed to get her hands on all sorts of other literature. Among her first favorites were fairy tales by the Brothers Grimm. "The grimmer the better," she recalled. "I loved gruesome gothic tales and, in that respect, I liked Bible stories, because to me they were very gothic. It's very gothic to have a little boy killing a giant, somebody's head being served on a platter, dead people being raised out of the grave."

She worked her way through all of Laura Ingalls Wilder's novels about life on the Great Plains—*Little House on the Prairie, Little House in the Big Woods,* and *By the Shore of Silver Lake.* As she mastered reading more difficult books, she also discovered that books could meet her need to be in control: she could defy her parents by seeming to study but really be disobeying. For instance, although forbidden by her parents to read J. D. Salinger's book about a troubled teenager, *The Catcher in the Rye,* Amy managed to obtain a copy of the prohibited book anyway, and she feasted on it.

Gradually, however, the young girl began to resign herself to believing that she would never be able to please her parents. But although she may have been learning how to cope with a sense of falling short, apparently her older brother Peter could not accept such a defeat.

A brilliant, high-achieving student at school, Peter encountered a crisis that he could not accept. The teenager had written an English paper that a friend copied and submitted as his own. The teacher punished both boys, failing them not just on the paper but for the entire semester. Peter was devastated, not only by the humiliation of the whole incident, but also, Amy believes, by a "total disillusionment about

Literature helped Amy define and control her personal world. She often defied her parents by reading forbidden books like Catcher in the Rye *by J. D. Salinger (pictured here).*

the consequences that are meted out in life. I suppose if my brother had become older it would have transmogrified into something different and made it a strength in his life, a turning point. [Instead] he despaired, and he went into depression and he began to sleep a lot."

Not long afterward, both Peter and his father were diagnosed with brain tumors. They were treated with chemotherapy, and Amy, her mother, and her brother John spent a year shuttling back and forth to hospitals. But the treatments didn't work. They died within six months of each other.

Amy was 15 when John and Peter Tan died. Her mother believed that somehow evil influences supposedly left behind in China had found the Tans again in the United States and caused this disaster. It was time to run away again.

Daisy Tan believed supernatural forces were at work on the Tan family. She packed up and moved the entire family to Europe over the protests of Amy. The Tans finally settled in Montreaux, Switzerland (shown here). It turned out to be a stroke of luck for Amy.

2

DECIDING
TO BE BAD

"I was raised the Chinese way: I was taught to desire nothing, to swallow other people's misery, to eat my own bitterness."

—from *The Joy Luck Club*

The deaths of John and Peter Tan in 1967 and 1968 reawakened Daisy's dread of malignant supernatural forces, which she believed were at work around them. She told Amy and her younger brother John that their home in Santa Clara was "diseased" and there was something wrong with the neighborhood itself. She further announced that to counteract these unhealthy influences, the remaining family members would relocate to a place that, perhaps to Daisy's mind, was the most remote fortress imaginable—central Europe. "We thought she was crazy," Amy said.

The Tans had already moved half a dozen times in California; they had lived in Oakland, Fresno, Berkeley, and other suburbs of San Francisco before settling in Santa Clara. Yet, ignoring her daughter's protests about moving once again,

Daisy took her two children in tow and led them to Europe.

Like gypsies, the Tans wandered through the Netherlands and Germany in a Volkswagen, looking for three things—a furnished home, an American school, and a location where Daisy felt secure. Finally, Daisy Tan settled on a spot: Montreaux, Switzerland.

But by a stroke of luck—or perhaps it was an example of Daisy's impulse to survive—Montreaux proved to be a good place in one sense for Amy. For a young woman who never felt she fit in, the American school she and her brother attended was a gathering point for the children of an assortment of international businesspeople and politicians. "They were *all* different," Amy said of the students attending Institut Monte Rosa Internationale. Being a stranger in a strange land was for once a normal condition among all the kids Amy knew.

No doubt Daisy felt that she was getting things fairly well in hand, despite the tragedy that had struck her family. By extension, she also looked for signs that Amy's disobedient spirit would somehow diminish because of the suffering they had all endured together. She thought that Amy would become a better daughter because of what had happened, but instead the young teenager became extremely rebellious.

As if wanting to escape everything she had ever known, Amy reinvented herself in Switzerland, becoming like the mountain-ringed nation itself with few loyalties outside its own borders. She recalled that once she was away from everybody who had known her in California she changed— from being, in her own words, a "nerdy little girl" into "a wild thing." The teenager who had gone to church every day and who had regularly attended Bible study, choir practice, and youth sessions began to hang around with an unruly crowd and started smoking and drinking.

Piling yet another shock on her mother, Amy got herself her first boyfriend, too. The 16-year-old began dating a German man who was 24. Everything about the man angered Daisy—he was too old to be dating a 16-year-old, had deserted from the German army, and had an illegitimate child. Amy continued to see him, and delighted in irritating her mother.

For Daisy Tan, her daughter's behavior was deliberately disrespectful and intolerable. She harangued the wayward Amy about her lack of gratitude, predicting that shame would be the result of disobeying her mother. Listening to her, Amy vowed, "I'm not going to have anything to do with anything Chinese when I leave home. I'm going to be completely American.' None of that Chinese torture or guilt ever again in my life. None of that responsibility crap, 'You owe it to your family. You have to do this for your family.'"

Amy retaliated with a new strategy designed to rob her mother of the satisfaction of even getting a response. During Daisy's anguished lectures, Amy gave her mother what she later described as "this stone face—no emotions. I wanted to prove that I could be the baddest of the bad. I couldn't wait until I could leave the house. I thought, 'I'll divorce myself from this family and never see her again.'"

Despite Amy's effort at concealing her emotions, however, they were still at war, roiling inside her. She hadn't really left her childhood religious upbringing behind: "There is one side of me that wanted to behave and to hear a voice that was God's voice saying, 'Amy, I have a mission for you. You are going to go out and save this country.' . . . I think the rebellious side came about because I thought I was

Amy's behavior was deliberately disrespectful; when she was 16 she began dating a 24-year-old German army deserter. Her mother responded with stern lectures about Amy's disrespect and lack of gratitude.

never going to hear the voice of God. I'd never be good enough for God or for my family or for my mother or father so I might as well be bad. And that I could succeed in."

The German boyfriend continued to be a flash-point between mother and daughter, even though Tan claims that the relationship involved nothing more than exchanged kisses. It was her first romance, she later explained, and she found the relationship very exciting, although even at the time she knew the man wasn't really the right person for her. She recalls that he wrote "beautiful love poetry" that made her feel very special.

Amy dismissed her mother's protests about the relationship as yet another ridiculous display of Daisy's being old world Chinese. Looking back on the event as an adult, though, Tan recognizes that she made a mistake in thinking her mother was over-protective because she was Chinese:

> If my mother didn't want me to date boys out of fear that somehow I would lose myself to this boy and ruin my life, I chalked up all of her fears to Chinese fears, not generational ones. Anything that was unreasonable, I said was Chinese so I made the culture the scapegoat. That's unfortunate, because it made me grow up wanting to deny that part of my family, of myself. Anything that was Chinese about me made me feel ashamed. I wanted to bury it so that what I thought was the stronger, more independent, American side could come out.

But if Amy believed it was her mother's culture blinding her to the truth about things, she failed to count on Daisy's resourcefulness, grown strong over a lifetime of having to face obstacles. Mrs. Tan hired a private detective, who learned that the German boyfriend hadn't just deserted from the German army; he had escaped from its mental hospital. The detective also established that the boyfriend was connected with drugs, and with that information Daisy Tan had her daughter arrested and hauled before the local magistrate. The fright caused by the drug arrest went deep. Amy recalls being terribly shocked: "I thought my life was over then, that all chances of ever going to college—of having a decent life, of being respected—were gone."

Later, Daisy drove her daughter to the Swiss border so she could see the boyfriend one last time before he was returned to Germany. The meeting proved enlightening; it allowed the defiant teen to realize that the relationship was over. Amy really didn't need or want to see the man anymore.

Also about this time, inconsolably enraged by her daughter's behavior—to the point of even threatening suicide—Mrs. Tan dropped a second bombshell. She told her wayward daughter that Amy was not her only daughter. When Daisy had lived in China, she explained, she had been married to a man who had abused her, and they had eventually divorced. However, the marriage had produced three daughters who were still living in China. According to Daisy, these girls had been good, obedient daughters who loved their mother and would have never treated her as Amy had.

The revelation had an unexpected effect on Amy—leaving her emotionally torn. She feared that her mother would leave her for those good Chinese daughters. However, she also recalled thinking in anger, "'Good, well you should go back to them!'" The pain of all that had happened—the death of her father and brother, the uprooting from the United States to Switzerland, the arrest for drugs, and the ongoing, constant quarreling with her mother—welled up and rushed forth in physical symptoms: "I was sick to my stomach, literally. I had dry heaves, and the pain was so enormous that at one point," said Tan, "when I thought I was going to die, I just suddenly realized that that scared me. And it was scary to live but it was scarier to die."

I remember just saying, "I want to live, I want to live, I want to live."

Daisy Tan moved the family back to the San Francisco Bay area after Amy's graduation from high school in 1969. Daisy already had Amy's next step planned—enrollment in Linfield College, a small, Baptist institution.

3

SEARCHING
FOR A PURPOSE

"My mother was convinced she had lost me. I was so determined not to have anything to do with her."

—Amy Tan, in a 1989 interview with *The New York Times*

Despite the uproar at home created by her fling with the drug-dealing, German boyfriend, Amy graduated in 1969 from her Switzerland high school—a year early. She and her mother and brother, John, returned to the San Francisco Bay Area, perhaps because the turmoil had soured them on living abroad. On the other hand, Daisy had the next phase in Amy's life already planned, which was attending college back in the United States. And she even had a school already picked out: Linfield College in McMinnville, Oregon.

To a devoted and determined single mother like Daisy, widowed at a crucial time in her children's lives—and with a daughter who was giving her a lot of trouble—Linfield probably appeared to be the perfect choice. Located in a small community, an hour from the city of Portland and the Oregon Coast, Linfield consisted of a 193-acre campus of green lawns, groves of trees, and conservative Georgian-style buildings. One of the oldest colleges on the West Coast, it had been founded as Baptist College in 1858. Daisy Tan's late husband had been a Baptist minister, and Linfield's connection to the faith, plus its quiet setting, must have seemed to Daisy like the right environment for her headstrong 17-year-old daughter.

Instead, Amy lasted only two semesters at Linfield. In 1970, she transferred to San Jose City College in California to be with her new Italian-American boyfriend, Louis DeMattei. She had met Lou, who was attending law school at San Jose University, on a blind date.

Amy's mother was so angry by this new development, which she considered yet another of her daughter's acts of defiance, that she refused to speak to her for six months. Amy made no overtures to break the silence. During that period of simmering warfare with her mother, Amy was convinced her mother's traditional Chinese values were suffocating her, she later told an interviewer. It would take years for her to recognize that the issues between the two of them had nothing to do with Chinese culture. Much of what happened between them occurred because of the relationships within her family and the personality of her mother.

More conflict was in store, however. After enrolling at San Jose City College, Amy switched her major from pre-med to a double major in English and linguistics—the study of language. Her mother was at a loss to understand this unwelcome news, too. "I remember her saying something about how disappointed my father would be," Tan told a writer for the *Washington Post*. "If I said I was going to be a physicist, or president of a bank, it would have been different. But I said I was going to be an English major. She could see nothing in that as a future." Daisy tried to resign herself to Amy's insistence at doing things her way, although the widening emotional distance between the two was hard for her to accept.

Amy's decision to switch to English and linguistics was a courageous one, as it turned out, and the first inkling of her true direction in life, although she was still of two minds about her future. She had dreamed of becoming an artist or writer when she was a little girl, recalling her happiness at winning the essay contest when she was eight, but she also considered such ideas as preposterous. Probably for that reason, she stuck to her double major in English and linguistics, but never took a single course in creative writing. Later, in an essay entitled "Mother Tongue," which appeared in *The Best American Essays 1991,* she would speculate that her reluctance to embrace writing as a career was influenced by the fact that she was raised in a household in which English was not her parents' language:

> I think my mother's [poor] English almost had an effect on limiting my possibilities in life. . . . While my English skills were never judged as poor, compared to math, English could not be considered my strong suit. . . . This was understandable. Math is precise; there is only one correct answer. Whereas, for me at least, the answers on English tests were always a judgment call, a matter of opinion and personal experience. . . . Fortunately, I happen to be rebellious in nature and enjoy the challenge of disproving assumptions made about me.

Yet, after the mother and daughter began speaking again, Amy's self-doubts would rear up anew whenever her mother, during heated arguments, reminded her that there were "good Chinese daughters" whom Daisy had left behind in China. They were not like her rebellious American-born daughter. Although Amy tried to dismiss whatever her mother was threatening as ridiculous, still it made her worry about going too far in challenging her mother's wishes—like being a writer instead of a doctor—or else her mother might stop loving her as a punishment. "I was afraid that because of her good Chinese daughters she would

Amy majored in English and linguistics instead of pre-med. Her mother reminded her of how disappointed her father would have been. This courageous switch turned out to be the first inkling of Amy's true direction in life.

drop me, her bad Chinese daughter," Amy recalled.

After transferring from San Jose City College to San Jose State University, Tan graduated with honors in 1972, receiving a bachelor's degree with a double major in English and linguistics, an unusual accomplishment in three years, and a demonstration of her trademark hard work. She was awarded a scholarship to attend the Summer Linguistics Institute at the University of California, Santa Cruz. Then in 1973, she earned a master's degree in linguistics, also from San Jose State University, and was awarded a graduate minority fellowship to pursue doctoral work at the University of California.

In 1974, Amy Tan and Lou DeMattei were married. She once recalled her first impression of her husband: "I was lucky that I met a very kind person, a very good person and that person is now my husband. He is a very sweet man. I wasn't in love with him when I first met him, but I knew he was a good person. I said, 'This is the kind of person my father was.'"

DeMattei had graduated from law school and taken up the practice of tax law. Meanwhile Tan studied for a doctorate in linguistics, first at the University of California Santa Cruz campus, then later at U.C. Berkeley.

Now in her 20s, and steeped in education about literature, language, and culture, Amy was no more certain about some aspects of herself than she had ever been. Where were all the classes, tests, and final papers leading? Why did she feel a sense of unease about her place in life, she wondered. Then, during the second year of her doctoral program at Berkeley, a personal loss shocked her into thinking about her life even more urgently.

A close friend of Amy and her husband Lou was murdered during a robbery. The sudden violent death shook Amy up: "I had plenty of time to think," she recalled. "Here was this person who had wonderful intentions to help other people and he was killed. And here I was doing crossword puzzles. What was I really doing with my life?"

Tan dropped out of graduate school and found a job as a language-development consultant to the Alameda County Association for Retarded Citizens. Later she directed a training project for developmentally disabled children. She supervised projects, helped fund-raise, planned activities, and taught. However, although she loved the work, the emotional stress and frustration of the job finally wore her down.

She resigned after four years, deciding to try something different yet again, something this time that would be a better fit with who she was. Meanwhile, she took a job for a few years working as an editor for a medical journal.

Then a friend suggested they go into a partnership together writing speeches, pamphlets, and brochures for businesses. Remembering the essay contest she had won as a child and the wonderful sense of accomplishment that had come with it, Amy didn't hesitate to accept the offer.

"I always wanted to be a writer," Amy told an interviewer from the New York Times. *After a few years as a freelance business writer, she had earned enough to buy her mother a house.*

4

THE WORKAHOLIC
TURNED WRITER

"When I was trying to write this thing [The Joy Luck Club], *my main concerns were so very basic: 'What is voice? What is the story about?'"*

—Amy Tan, from a 1989 interview with the *New York Times*

"I had always wanted to be a writer," Tan once told an interviewer for the *New York Times*. "I used to write little fantasy stories to myself. Sometimes I wrote these stories to friends in the guise of a letter. But I also had the practical sense that a person doesn't make a lot of money being a writer, and I couldn't do that except as an indulgence, as a hobby."

But in the early 1980s, with a partner whose expertise was business writing, Tan saw that it was possible to make money and be a writer. Together she and her partner landed accounts from clients who wanted what might be called popular technical writing—explanations of business concepts couched in an easy-to-read style. The work required them to produce speeches for business executives and text for brochures and booklets.

Unfortunately, the partnership broke down not long after it started. Tan later explained that she and her partner had signed papers to set up their joint company, and she had already put many long hours into the business. However, one day they disagreed over her role—she wanted to do more writing and he insisted that her talents were in project management. That job involved tasks such as taking care of clients, making estimates, hiring contractors, and collecting bills—none of which interested Amy. She wanted to write, but her business partner insisted that writing was her weakest skill.

Tan became angry and demanded that she be treated as an equal partner. Her friend responded that she was not an equal partner because the legal papers for their business had never been finalized. Amy threatened to quit on the spot. In an interview with the Academy of Achievement, she recalled how her business partner then scoffed and said, "So what do you think you're going to do?"

"I'm going to freelance write," Tan replied confidently.

"Oh, fat chance," he said. "You'll be lucky to make a dime."

"With that sendoff into the world," Tan remembered, "I was determined to make it as a writer. I worked day and night trying to build my business, writing a business plan and thinking of how I could do this. So in that sense, it was adversity that made me force myself to be successful in that kind of business writing."

Amy did become successful, throwing herself into the work with characteristic energy and determination. The young woman who had graduated early from both high school and college pushed herself hard to build a business in record time. Before long,

Amy worked day and night on her freelance writing business. Her clients included companies such as AT&T, IBM, and Pacific Bell.

she was a business writer on her own, specializing in corporate communications for such companies as AT&T, IBM, and Pacific Bell. Within a few years— as if calling anyone's bluff about her ability to write and make money—she earned enough money that she could buy her mother a house.

"My mother started feeling that maybe I was doing okay for myself when I became successful as a freelance business writer and my husband and I were able to buy her a place to live," she said in an interview for *Poets & Writers Magazine*. "That's really what success is about in Chinese families—it's not success for yourself, it's success so you can take care of your family."

But success never seemed to be a destination she could arrive at—just an ideal slightly beyond her grasp. She ratcheted-up the pressure on herself to achieve even more, deciding she would increase the amount of money that she made. Her goal simply became to have more and more work—more billable hours—for each subsequent month. By the end of her third year of being a freelance writer, she was billing 90 hours a week.

With that kind of working schedule, Tan had quickly become a workaholic. She had no time to sleep. And she came to realize that she had no real life either. Even though she was attaining success with the growing list of top-notch clients, and making a great deal of money, she also realized that she wasn't happy and didn't feel satisfied.

Amy decided to counterbalance her need to work by taking up a creative outlet—teaching herself to play jazz piano. She had learned how to play the instrument as a child, when her parents had hoped for a concert pianist in the family. Perhaps, she thought, she could find enjoyment in playing the piano if she did it just for herself.

In the meantime, her mother Daisy had returned to China for the first time in more than 30 years, since fleeing Shanghai just ahead of the Communists in the late 1940s. Amy admits that she felt threatened by her mother's journey, certain that when Daisy Tan reunited with her three "good Chinese daughters," they would at last take up center stage in her affections, leaving Amy devastated in the wings.

But to her near astonishment and relief, nothing like that happened. "[My mother] would write me letters from China, telling me about my sisters, about how China was now. I was so grateful that she still loved me, and I became much more interested [in the country]," Tan remembered during an interview with the *Philadelphia Inquirer Sunday Magazine*. Daisy returned from her trip excited and happy to see Amy again.

But despite mother and daughter growing closer, the pattern of Amy's workaholism didn't change. She accepted practically all the work that was offered to her, believing, as freelance writers tend to do, that the opportunity might dry up at any second, or that she couldn't afford to disappoint anyone by not taking on the assignments offered. She would see a therapist to help her overcome her inability before she could say no to the extra work.

The treatment didn't go well. Whenever Amy drove herself to tears describing something terrible from her childhood—the deaths from brain tumors of her father and brother, her loneliness, the arguments she had with her mother—the therapist became interested. Otherwise, he seemed bored, she thought. The third time he fell asleep during one of their sessions, she quit.

Besides, something else had grabbed her attention—reading fiction. After immersing herself in the works of Eudora Welty, Flannery O'Connor, and Alice Munro, Amy found herself fascinated by Louise Erdrich's novel *Love Medicine*. Tan was so impressed by the power of its interlocking stories about another cultural minority—Native Americans—that she decided to try writing short stories herself.

At first, Amy tried writing the kind of stories that she thought other people would want to read. For instance, she wrote stories about families who were wealthy or whose members were well-educated professors at Massachusetts Institute of Technology or Harvard. She would later admit that by choosing such subjects, she was really trying to copy somebody else's style rather than create her own. She said that she had to learn "there is something called originality and your own voice."

Finally, after being told one of her stories didn't work because it seemed to have an inauthentic voice narrating it, Tan decided, "I'm just going to stop showing my work to people, and I'm just going to write a story. Make it fictional, but they'll be Chinese-American." This change in attitude provided the breakthrough in her writing as she began to listen to her own thoughts and speak in her own voice—and that of her mother.

One of the stories that tumbled out amazed her: "I wrote about a girl who plays chess and her mother is both her worst adversary and her best ally. I didn't play chess, so I figured that counted for fiction, but I made her Chinese-American, which made me a little uncomfortable. By the end of this story I was practically crying. Because I realized that—although it was fiction and none of that had ever happened to me in that story—it was the closest thing of describing my life." she said.

In 1985 this short story, entitled "Endgame," earned Amy an invitation to join the Squaw Valley Community of Writers, a fiction writers' workshop run by novelist Oakley Hall of the University of California at Irvine. Through the workshop she met author Molly Giles, who helped Tan rewrite and polish "Endgame," as well as other stories. Giles would later lead a small writing workshop that often met in Tan's house.

Writing "Endgame" helped Tan discover one of the main reasons for creating fiction—as a way to provide therapeutic release for the writer. "Through that, this subversion of myself, of creating something that never happened, I came closer to the truth," Amy explained in an interview with the American Academy of Achievement. "So, to me, fiction became a process of discovering what was true, for me. Only for me."

Sharing her work with the writers in the workshop,

Fiction writing grabbed Amy's attention. Her fiction became better when she began to write in a Chinese-American voice. Her story "Endgame" (depicted here in a scene from The Joy Luck Club) *was about a chess-playing girl whose mother is both her worst adversary and her ally.*

however, Amy found that she had almost too much she wanted to say. Giles read over her work and told her, "There's so many things that are happening that are not working, but there's a possible beginning. If I were you, I would start over again and take each one of these and make that your story. You don't have one story here, you have 12 stories. Sixteen stories,'" Tan recalled.

After some intensive editing and rewriting, Amy submitted "Endgame" to a local literary magazine, *FM Five*. It was accepted and published, but more importantly, it was picked up and reprinted by *Seventeen* magazine, where it found its way into the hands of Sandra Dijkstra, a literary agent in Del Mar, California. Dijkstra was so impressed she contacted Tan. But the freshly minted writer of short stories remained skeptical.

Dijkstra offered to become Tan's agent, and encouraged her to keep writing. Amy explained that she couldn't pay an agent, but she was told any fees were on a commission basis—nothing would be charged unless Dijkstra sold Tan's stories. Doubtful that such an event would come to pass, Amy nevertheless sent a few more stories to the agent, who then requested synopses of more stories, as well as a proposed outline that incorporated the tales in a book.

But Tan had more important things on her mind. In 1986, the same year "Endgame" was published in *Seventeen*, her mother was hospitalized with an apparent heart attack. The possibility that her mother might die—*would* die eventually, of course—made Amy rethink her priorities. She decided that if her mother improved and was well enough to travel, she would get to know her better. Amy established new goals for herself: to travel with her mother to China, and to write a book.

Tan promised her mother they would go to China together once she recovered. And true to Amy's word, the following year, in 1987, they embarked for the land of their shared ancestry, but not before Amy had first delivered to her persistent agent, Sandra Dijkstra, a complete proposal for a book of stories.

In 1987, Amy traveled with her mother to China. Though nervous about spending three weeks with her mother, Amy knew the trip would give her the opportunity to both learn about her family and meet her half-sisters.

5

JOURNEY TO CHINA

"When my feet touched China, I became Chinese. I knew I was not totally Chinese, but I felt the connection nevertheless. It was a sense of completeness, like having a mother and a father. I had China and America, and everything was all coming together finally."

—Amy Tan, from a 1989 interview with *The New York Times*

As the time drew near to leave for China, Amy grew increasingly nervous. She was concerned about how she would get along with her mother during the trip, she later explained, "It meant three weeks with my mother, and I had hardly spent more than a couple of hours alone with her in the last 20 years." But Tan recognized that taking the journey would give her the opportunity to better understand both herself and her mother. It would also give Amy the opportunity to understand Daisy Tan's past—where she had lived, the family members who had raised her, and the daughters she had left behind.

The China that Daisy Tan was returning to with her American-born daughter was not the China of 1949, the year Daisy had fled. It was blossoming after being repressed for almost 30 years, slightly more than the length of Amy's life at the time, under the triple weight of Communism, dictatorship, and xenophobia—fear of outsiders.

Since the death of Mao Tse-tung in September 1976—the leader of the Communist revolution in 1949 and China's unquestioned dictator ever since—the nation had been slowly entering the world scene. Now a more liberal government, under the leadership of reformer Deng Xiaoping, was turning its attention to correcting China's economic and technological backwardness, the result of decades of isolation from the Western world.

Deng and the other moderates sought to reduce the Chinese people's admiration of Mao Tse-tung. Many people admired Mao so much that they believed China should follow all his policies. The moderates praised Mao's leadership, but denounced the idea that all his policies should be followed. Instead, they were greatly increasing trade and cultural contact with foreign countries. They sought to modernize China's economy with technical help from abroad.

Not all mainland Chinese welcomed this second revolution in the course of one lifetime, however. Many worried that China's traditions would be eroded away by an avalanche of Western values. In fact, like a thunderbolt striking the population, it suddenly became fashionable in China in the early 1980s to learn and adopt Western ways—particularly American ways. So rapid was the pace of change in China that a serious suggestion was made to abandon Chinese characters for writing and use the English alphabet instead, because it was the language of computers (Chinese software has since made that unnecessary).

Amy's trip to China helped her discover a place where she belonged and felt at home with history. She discovered how American she was, but also how Chinese she was. These revelations helped her put her life in perspective.

Unknowingly then, but appropriately too, Daisy and Amy Tan in 1987 mirrored the new China. On the one hand was Daisy, a woman whose childhood and youth was steeped in centuries-old lore, traditions, values, and beliefs. On the other was Amy, a thoroughly American woman who nevertheless felt the pull of old China strongly on her.

During the trip, Amy learned that her mother was just as critical and argumentative in China as she was in the United States. This knowledge provided inspiration for scenes from The Joy Luck Club, *shown here.*

The moment of Amy's arrival changed her, she said. She explained that once she touched Chinese soil, she better understood her connection to the land and to the country. In addition, she believes visiting China helped her understand how she could be the product of two cultures at the same time, finding her own level of comfort where she needed it: "I discovered how American I was. I also discovered how Chinese I was by the kind of family habits and routines that were so familiar. I discovered a sense of finally belonging to a period of history, which I never felt with American history," she explained in an interview with the Academy of Achievement.

"When you read about the Civil War," she explained, "a lot of people, like my husband, can say [his] great-great-grandfather fought in that war. . . . but I could never imagine my ancestors having been in any of this history because my parents came to this country in 1949. So none of that history before then seemed relevant to me. It was wonderful going to a country where suddenly the landscape, the geography, the history was relevant. That was enormously important to me."

More revelations were in store, but these had to do with seeing her mother in a new setting, too. Since early childhood, Amy had ascribed her mother's behavior to one thing—being Chinese in America made her a difficult person. That was not so, as it turned out. Before the trip to China, Amy had thought her mother got into arguments with people because they didn't understand her English, because she was Chinese. She learned that her mother's personality was such that in China she often got into arguments with Chinese people as well. The language being spoken made no difference.

And then there were the insights to be gained from being around her half-sisters and seeing her mother interact with them. Amy could see the similarities that she and her half-sisters had inherited from their mother. And her half-sisters also learned some things about their mother that Amy had known all along. She laughed as she recalled that her half-sisters "had grown up thinking that they had been denied this wonderful, loving, nurturing mother who would have understood everything and been sweet and kind and never would have criticized them. Well suddenly they were shocked to find this mother saying, 'You didn't cook this long enough,' or 'This is too salty,' and 'Why do you wear that? It makes you look terrible.' They were shocked, too."

For so long, Amy had assumed that she as a daughter had fallen short somehow; that her anger toward her mother was ungrateful and mean-spirited. But watching her half-sisters respond with bewilderment and defensiveness to their mother's remarks helped her realize that Daisy Tan was who she was, whether in the United States, Switzerland, or China. The half-sisters were just like Amy—daughters who wanted their mother's approval, and didn't understand why she was so critical.

The trip was a success in ways that Amy could never have anticipated, but especially because it helped her see her mother in a brand-new perspective. And the timing of her exposure to China couldn't have been better, as it turned out. When she returned, her agent Sandra Dijkstra called with exciting news. She'd sold the book proposal to a major publisher, G. P. Putnam's Sons.

"What book?" Tan asked, confused. The outline for the book of stories, she was reminded, based on ones like "Endgame" and another she'd written called "Waiting Between the Trees." The amount the publisher was offering as an advance—a commitment between author and publisher—was $50,000.

When Amy learned of the offer, she was "flabbergasted," she later admitted to the *New York Times*. She immediately dropped her freelancing, and as is her style, plunged headlong into working overtime on the stories she'd promised, from 7:30 A.M. every day to well past dinner time.

For inspiration, Amy often called upon the feelings

she experienced while in China. She recalled the stream of stories, remarks, and images that her mother and aunt had shared over the years while Amy was growing up; she had listened to their murmuring talk in the background, barely interested yet somehow absorbing much of the conversation. She recalled the anecdotes her mother told her, such as one about a friend who was fleeing from the Japanese in the war. The woman had been carrying several bags in her hands as she fled, but eventually began dropping them along the road, one by one. The scene replayed itself in the book in a story about a woman who, after dropping bags of necessities and food by the roadside as she fled, came to the point of exhaustion where she put her two babies down and left them, too.

Every day, as the writing work went on, Amy followed a routine designed to put her into a receptive state of mind for telling stories with magical overtones. She recalled the environment she would create before beginning to write: "I'd light incense, put on certain music and start to imagine myself in another world. I conjured up people to come and tell me their stories. Then I'd enter that other world and hours would go by and I'd forget everything else."

Once she immersed herself in the storytelling voice of her mother and aunt, Amy felt as if she were taking dictation. She would later reveal in an interview that when she wrote her stories, she felt as if she were actually reading them for the first time, that it seemed that other people were telling her the stories, not that she herself was writing them. She was just listening and writing down the tales as she heard them. Then she would revise each one, at least 20 times, before putting it aside to move on to the next one.

As Amy worked, she came to realize the stories

Anecdotes from Amy's mother and aunt helped provide inspiration for Amy's writing. The story of a woman forced to drop her possessions, including her babies, as she fled the Japanese, was depicted in The Joy Luck Club.

were not just her mother's, either, but *for* her mother, too. She explained her goal: "I wanted [my mother] to know what I thought about China and what I thought about growing up in this country. And I wanted those words to almost fall off the page so that she could just see the story, that the language would be simple enough, almost like a little curtain that would fall away."

At last, after four months of writing, the stories were done. She submitted the manuscript to Dijkstra to deliver to the publisher. The title was *The Joy Luck Club*.

Amy poses with her best friend, Gretchen Shields, who also illustrated the cover of The Joy Luck Club.

6

THE JOY LUCK CLUB AND SUCCESS

"The success took me by surprise and it frightened me. On the day that there was a publication party for my book, I spent the whole day crying. I was scared out of my mind that my life was changing and it was out of my control and I didn't know why it was happening."

—Amy Tan, from an interview with the American Academy of Achievement

While Amy Tan had been working on her story collection, she had to fight down the suspicion that perhaps what was happening was too good to be true. Later, in an interview with *Newseek* magazine, she recalled wondering whether her publisher's interest was "all a token minority thing. I thought they had to fill a quota since there weren't many Chinese-Americans writing."

Nevertheless, when *The Joy Luck Club* manuscript arrived in the offices of G. P. Putnam's Sons in 1987, it bore her trademark signs of hard work, devotion to the task, and thoroughness. According to Faith Sale, the editor at Putnam who had offered

$50,000 for Tan's manuscript, two typewritten copies of the manuscript, "clean as anything you've ever seen, in perfect white boxes, imprinted with the 'Joy Luck' chop [symbol] Amy's mother had encouraged her to have made while in China and tied with red ribbon—the Chinese color for good luck—arrived on time by the middle of May."

Sale had offered the sum to Tan after seeing only three sample stories, an outline of the rest, and a promise from agent Sandra Dijkstra that the young author from San Francisco was the genuine article: an undiscovered author with real potential. There was always the chance that Amy, despite the quality of the sample stories, might not be able to go the distance—might not be able to produce a collection that merited a book. But as Sale read the finished manuscript, she realized that she had been right to take a risk. As she later told the book trade publication, *Publishers Weekly*, "This is storytelling on a pure level, about mothers and daughters, with universal appeal. Second, the book gets in so very close to people; it's so intimate, it seems as though Amy is telling the story just to you."

Word circulated around the offices of Putnam that an exceptionally good book was in the works, and several publicists on staff, whose job it would be to promote the new title, vied for the job. The responsibility went to Jill Bernstein. She read the manuscript in one sitting, and from the pleasure of the experience found herself reminded, she recalled, of why she got into the publishing business. She also knew a winner for publicity purposes when she saw one, believing the book was a strong contender for receiving good reviews and a fair amount of coverage in the media, as well as potential for being featured at bookstore readings. And finally, Amy had already shown herself willing to help publicize the book—a cooperative spirit that every publisher is grateful for, because bringing out a new book costs a great deal of money, even before the first copy is sold. Bernstein heard that Amy had actually videotaped scenes of herself and her husband at a Joy Luck Club meeting in Chinatown; Putnam would later use the tape at its sales conference to introduce the book.

Believing the book could be a best-seller, the publishing house moved quickly to guarantee maximum exposure. Rights were sold to the Book of the Month Club in September to offer *The Joy Luck Club* as one of its choices. Serial rights were sold the following month to the *Atlantic, Ladies' Home Journal,* and *San Francisco Focus.* Audio rights were sold to Dove Entertainment, which later issued a cassette of Tan reading the stories. Foreign markets were not overlooked, either. The giant Italian publishing house Rizzoli purchased the rights to issue its own edition, as did other publishers in France, Holland, Japan, Sweden, and Israel.

The publicity wave swept over Amy, as well—a facet of publishing that some authors enjoy and others dread. From the solitude of her basement writing nook where she had crafted her stories, Tan was suddenly summoned into the glare of the national limelight, as Putnam mailed 458 bound galleys, or early publication copies, to magazine and newspaper editors, and program directors at television and radio stations. Dozens of periodicals interviewed her, including *People, Esquire, Fortune,* and the *Los Angeles Times.* She was interviewed three times on National Public Radio, once each on CBS Radio and the Voice of America network, and on various local stations and syndicates across the United States and Canada.

Dan Harvey, associate publisher at Putnam, remarked to *Publishers Weekly,* "Over the years I have worked with many very talented novelists, but I never saw the kind of unanimous positive response to a first work of fiction that this book got."

The "buzz," as they say in the media, was clearly building. A graphic artist friend of Tan's, Gretchen Schields, provided a striking book-cover illustration of twisting dragons and fan-shaped designs in Chinese-Tibetan style. For the launch period of early spring 1989, Putnam had planned to issue 25,000 copies but quickly revised the figure upward to 100,000.

And then, as if sending off the book with one final blessing on its way, Tan added a dedication to the source of its inspiration—her mother. "Before I wrote *The Joy Luck Club*," she told *People* magazine, "my mother said, 'I might die soon. And if I die, what will you remember?'" The dedication Tan penned in response was, "You asked me once what I would remember. This, and much more."

But no matter how much care an author, agent, and publisher put into the creation of a book, even up to the moment of its publication, another group of professionals act as counterbalance to their efforts—the book critics. A "thumbs down" from an influential reviewer for a respected newspaper or magazine can have a chilling effect on sales.

Instead, reviewers of *The Joy Luck Club* seemed to compete in ways to praise it. Said Carolyn See of *The Los Angeles Times*, "The only negative thing I could ever say about this book is that I'll never again be able to read it for the first time. *The Joy Luck Club* is so powerful, so full of magic, that by the end of the second paragraph, your heart catches; by the end of the first page, tears blur your vision, and one-third of the way down on Page 26, you know you won't be doing anything of importance until you have finished this novel."

Although called a novel, the book is really a collection of 16 interlocking tales that alternate between the stories of four Chinese immigrant mothers and those of their Chinese-American daughters: Suyuan

and Jing-mei "June" Woo, An-mei and Rose Hsu, Lindo and Waverly Jong, and Ying-ying and Lena St. Clair. The four Chinese mothers in San Francisco have gathered weekly at Joy Luck Club meetings since 1949 to play mah-jongg, eat Chinese food, and gossip about their children. (Daisy Tan was a member of just such a group).

In the story, Suyuan Woo is the founder of the Joy Luck Club, which she started in Chungking during the last of World War II when she was a young widow. Distraught by the scenes of horror taking

In Tan's book, later made into a film, the Joy Luck Club is composed of four aging "aunties" who have gathered regularly since 1949 to play mah-jongg, eat Chinese food, and gossip about their children.

place around her, she defiantly started the club with friends to create joy and luck out of catastrophe:

> What was worse, we asked among ourselves, to sit and wait for our own deaths with proper somber faces? Or to choose our own happiness?
>
> So we decided to hold parties and pretend each week had become the new year. Each week we could forget past wrongs done to us. We weren't allowed to think a bad thought. We feasted, we laughed, we played games, lost and won, we told the best stories. And each week, we could hope to be lucky. That hope was our only joy. And that's how we came to call our little parties Joy Luck.

After the fall of China to the Communists, Suyuan Woo emigrates to the United States, and starts up the club in San Francisco, where it continues for the next 40 years, a connection in spirit and history to the past. By sharing their stories at their weekly meetings, the

Joy Luck Club members keep contact with the lives, the people, and the beliefs that they were forced to leave behind in China.

When *The Joy Luck Club* begins, Suyuan Woo has died, and her Americanized daughter, Jing-Mei , has been asked to take her mother's place at the mah-jongg table and fill the empty chair. Tan explains that the club's three older women—Jing-Mei's aunties—represent "different aspects of my mother, but the book could be about any culture or generation and what is lost between them."

Jing-Mei is uncomfortable with being drafted to sit among the older women who meet in one another's houses, where "too many once fragrant smells" from Chinese cooking have been "compressed onto a thin layer of invisible grease." The meetings of the Joy Luck Club have always disturbed her as little more than a "shameful Chinese custom, like the secret gathering of the Ku Klux Klan or the tom-tom dances of TV Indians preparing for war."

On the other hand, Jing-Mei finds, she has an opportunity to learn more about her mother and herself by meeting with her three aunties. Her own life has been difficult for her—she has held several jobs and feels she has been settling for less than she should. Dissatisfied with herself, Jing-Mei believes her mother, Suyuan Woo, died bitterly disappointed in her.

During Jing-Mei's first night at the mah-jongg table, however, the three aunties tell her a secret that knocks down her rickety and inaccurate sense of self—they want to give her money so she can take a trip to China to visit her two sisters—daughters from an earlier marriage that her mother left behind when she fled the country. From then on, Jing-Mei supplies the main narrative that pulls together the tales told by mothers and daughters who sweep in and out of the book. In doing so, Jing-Mei constructs a new and authentic identity.

To provide a structure for presenting the tales—some pattern for helping the reader—Tan relies on the pattern of play in the game of mah-jongg itself, with the order of the stories coordinated by the rules of the game.

Although there are both Jewish and Chinese versions of mah-jongg, both begin the same way: four players begin with a pile of decorated tiles from which they each choose a starting set, much like dominoes. Chinese mah-jongg is organized by a seasonal motif in which the players represent the four winds that blow from the four compass directions. In *The Joy Luck Club,* each woman plays the position she wins by a roll of the dice.

In the first game that Jing-Mei plays, her partner, Lindo Jong, is East and plays first, then Ying-Ying St. Clair is South, An-Mei Hsu is West, and Jing-Mei is North, who plays last. Play ordinarily proceeds by the East player picking up fourteen tiles (because East is where the sun rises). Then play moves clockwise, with the players at South, West, and North picking up thirteen tiles each. East's advantage in tiles is balanced by two other customs: if she loses, she pays double, but if she wins, she wins double.

Because Tan is writing out of two traditions, Chinese and American, she uses "American rules" to tell her story. In the first set of stories, "Feathers from a Thousand *Li* Away, " she begins with the story of 36-year-old Jeng-Mei, who is taking her mother's place at the mah-jongg table and who starts as East. The mother's stories then follow, told by An-Mei Hsu (South), Lindo Jong (West), and Ying-Ying St. Clair (North).]

But when the mothers' rebellious daughters—Lena Jong, Waverly St. Clair, Rose Hsu Jordan, and Jing-Mei—tell their sides of stories in ""The Twenty-Six Malignant Gates," the starting place is repositioned and the order breaks down. Then, Tan reverses the order of play to go counterclockwise as each story displays

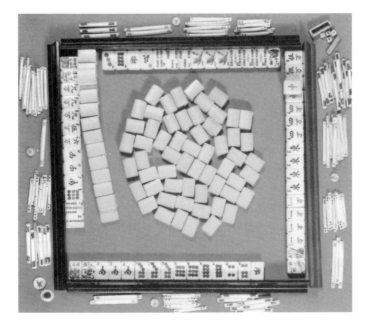

In Chinese mah-jongg, the four players represent winds from the east, west, north, and south. As with dominoes, players draw a starting set of tiles from a pile in the middle. Play proceeds in a clockwise fashion.

consequences of the daughters' rebellions.

Finally, in "Queen Mother from the Western Skies," Tan rotates once more and takes Jing-Mei home to China, a land she never knew except in stories.

The pattern not only gives step-by-step order to the storytelling, but in a larger sense, it mirrors the back-and-forth of the mother/daughter struggles taking place. *New York Times* reviewer Orville Schell wrote, "Moving back and forth across the divide between the two generations, the two continents and the two cultures, we find ourselves transported across the Pacific Ocean from the upwardly mobile, design-conscious, divorce-prone and Americanized world of the daughters in San Francisco to the world of China in the '20s and '30s, which seems more fantastic and dreamlike than real."

Reviewer Valerie Miner, writing in the *Nation*, also praised the book for its realism: "Tan has a remarkable ear for dialogue and dialect, representing the choppy English of the mothers and the sloppy California vernacular of the daughters with sensitive authenticity.

These stories are intricately seamed with the provocative questions about language that emerge from bilingual and trilingual homes."

On April 12, 1989, with sales of the book roaring toward the best-seller lists, Putnam held a 12-hour auction for rights among 10 major publishing houses to reprint *The Joy Luck Club* in paperback. Vintage Books submitted the winning bid—$1.2 million. That year, and into the following winter, Tan's first book logged more than 40 weeks on *The New York Times* list. It was nominated for the National Book Award and the National Book Critics Award. It received the Commonwealth Gold Award and the Bay Area Book Reviewers Award.

Tan also found out, however, that fame carries a price. The successful reception of *The Joy Luck Club* took her by surprise. And the sudden changes that she knew were about to take place frightened her. At that point, she later confessed, she had finally been feeling in control of her life and was terrified the newfound success could ruin things—whether her now-positive relationship with her mother or her longtime marriage. She recalled thinking, "We were happy, we had our first house, we had great friends, we were doing well, we weren't starving. We had a comfortable living and I thought, 'Things are going to get messed up here and I have no control over this.' I could already see how people were treating me differently. That's the scary thing."

In fact, despite her efforts to "keep everything the same," with her newfound success she and her husband were forced to make changes to defend their privacy. Although she and her husband lived in a comfortable home in San Francisco, it was on the first floor and she soon became aware that people were walking by every day, pointing at her home. She learned that the mailman would tell anyone who asked what mail she had received. So she and her husband Louis found a new place to live—on the third floor of a condominium.

Amy's first book spent more than 40 weeks on the New York Times *best-seller list; she received accolades and many award nominations. She also found that fame has a price: "The success took me by surprise and it frightened me," she said.*

Meanwhile, Daisy Tan was exulting over her daughter's success. "I'm so proud of Amy," Daisy Tan was quoted in *People*. "She's so talented—but maybe every mother says that." When *Newsweek* magazine asked Amy how her mother was responding to the successful publication of *The Joy Luck Club*, Amy said, "She's busy going to bookstores to see if they have the book. If they don't, she scolds them."

Amy became a celebrity after the publication of her first book. She relaxes here with her Yorkshire terrier, Mr. Bubba Zo.

7

THE 1990S—A DECADE OF WORK AND FAME

"By the time it came to the second book, I was so freaked out, I broke out in hives. I couldn't sleep at night. I broke three teeth grinding my teeth. I had backaches. I had to go to physical therapy. I was a wreck!"

—Amy Tan, from an interview with the
American Academy of Achievement

Despite the efforts of Amy and her husband, Lou, to maintain a reasonable amount of privacy in the wake of the success of *The Joy Luck Club*, she was a celebrity, her face recognizable to many people who read newsstand magazines like *People*, *Life*, or *Esquire*.

"In some ways it's like being a kid in a candy store," said Tan to a *New York Times* writer in 1991. "But there's also the loss of privacy. I'll be getting up from a nap on an airplane, and someone will come over to me and say, 'You're Amy Tan.' And I'll realize that I look like everybody else does when they've just awakened on a plane, and I want to say, 'No, I'm not.'"

But the pressures associated with being a public figure were small, by comparison, with the pressures Amy put on herself to write a second book, one that wouldn't disappoint editors, readers, and critics who hoped for a replay of her earlier success.

Not long after *The Joy Luck Club* had appeared, Tan was in New York having lunch with editor Faith Sale, who by now had become her closest friend, and another author who already had four books in print. The author asked Tan if she had started a second book.

Tan described the situation in an article she wrote for *Publishers Weekly* entitled, "Angst and the Second Novel":

> "I have some ideas," I said vaguely. I was loathe to admit in front of Faith that I had not the slightest idea what I would do next. "I just haven't decided which one to go with," I added. "All I know is that it won't be Son of Joy Luck."
>
> "Well, don't sweat over it too much," the other writer said. "The Second Book's doomed no matter what you do. Just get it over with, let the critics bury it, then move on to your third book and don't look back." I saw the bar graphs of my literary career falling over like headstones.

Amy's anxieties about whether she could deliver a repeat performance continued to mount. Seven times she started writing, producing 100 or 200 pages, by her own count, before giving up and throwing them away. She agonized, trying to discover what elements had made her first novel so popular, and determined to repeat them.

A nagging worry of hers was that she didn't want to be pegged as the expert on mother-daughter relationships. As a result, she consciously kept trying to work against the grain of *The Joy Luck Club*, until she realized that rebellion against a book was not a good reason to write. What she needed was inspiration, not a heavy sense of obligation or even desperation to get her ideas flowing again.

Once again, her mother Daisy provided the spark. "My mother kept complaining about how she had to tell everybody she was not the model for the mother in *The Joy Luck Club*," Amy explained in a *New York Times* interview. (Actually the author had drawn many elements of *The Joy Luck Club* from her relationship with her mother; however, Daisy's life was not the cornerstone of the book.) "She told me that next time I should write her true story."

Tan already knew the story of her mother's life in broad-brush strokes—that she had lived in China during World War II, had been married to an abusive man, and lost custody of her three daughters before fleeing to the United States—but Amy did not know how her mother had coped with the war. Although she had asked her mother what the war had been like, Amy had been told very little, and in fact Daisy Tan had claimed that she hadn't been affected by the war. Then she happened to mention one memory: there were frequent bombings of the city, perhaps two or three times a week, during which the people would flee to the city gates: "We were always running," she told Amy. "We were always scared that the bombs would fall on top of our heads."

Amy was confused. She asked her mother again how she could then say she wasn't affected by the war. Daisy's reply, according to Amy, was that she wasn't affected because she wasn't killed.

The matter-of-fact way that her mother put aside the war, as if she had defeated its power, astonished Tan. The contrast between her mother's view of what was important in life—surviving the near-breakdown of civilization—versus Amy's own, upper-middle class American outlook, opened the door to a new book. She wanted to try to capture that difference, she decided.

Although in the actual writing Tan changed some of the details of her mother's life for reasons of plot and

This destruction, known as the rape of Nanking, was part of the Japanese Imperial Army's invasion and occupation of China during World War II. Amy's mother lived in Nanking at the time.

drama, she kept her second book, *The Kitchen God's Wife*, published in 1991, as close as possible to Daisy Tan's experiences as she could. The book explores another troubled mother/daughter relationship as it tells the story of Winnie Louie, a Chinese woman living in San Francisco who has finally decided to share her tragic past—an abusive marriage, the loss of her children, being jailed, and a desperate flight to the United States—with her Americanized daughter, Pearl.

The Kitchen God's Wife follows many events that occurred in Daisy Tan's life. As Amy wrote the story, she found herself understanding her mother far more than she had before. "I realized that I had never really listened in the way she wanted someone to," Tan told a *New York Times* writer several years after *The Kitchen God's Wife* appeared. "She wanted someone to go back and relive her life with her. It was a way for her to exorcize her demons, and for me to finally listen and empathize and learn what memory means, and what you can change about the past."

Writing the book, Tan said, also enabled her to probe aspects of her mother's life—of most women's lives in old China—she had never understood. "She is such a strong person," Tan said. "And I could never understand why she lived with such a horrible man for 12 years of her life. She once told me that she might even kill him if she ever saw him again. If she hated him that much, why didn't she leave him? . . . And then I started thinking about all the different myths we grow up with, all the assumptions and the expectations. There are these things that form and control our lives that we never question." The novel's title refers to a Chinese myth about a man who wrongs his wife and is later elevated to the status of a deity.

One of Tan's relatives, however, was adamant that Daisy's past, and Amy's grandmother's past, should not have been revealed because it was shameful. Tan's grandmother was the woman in *The Kitchen God's Wife* who had been raped, been forced to be a concubine, and finally killed herself. Daisy Tan believed that she had carried shame in her life long enough, however, and it was indeed time to tell the world what had happened to her. Like Tan's first novel, *The Kitchen God's Wife* met positive reviews and quickly reached best-seller status.

For her next book, Amy tried a new genre, or category in the arts, and penned a children's storybook, *The Moon Lady,* published in 1992. In the story, 7-year-old Ying-ying attends an autumn moon festival in China. The young girl spends the day waiting to meet Lady Chang-o, who is believed to live on the moon and who once a year will grant the secret, unspoken wishes of the heart. The book was illustrated by her friend Gretchen Schields, who had designed the covers for *The Joy Luck Club* and *The Kitchen God's Wife*.

Tan had also been working on a third adult book, but oddly, instead of her second book failing to soar, this one—*The Year of No Flood*—never got off the ground. It was planned as a story set during the Chinese Boxer Rebellion in 1900 about a missionary from Ohio and a young Chinese boy. Amy said she was unable to finish it because she discovered, as countless authors have before, that talking too much about it in advance ruined the excitement of writing it. "It was like opening Christmas presents early and then having to go back later [and] act surprised. You try to rewrap it, but it's not the same," she said.

In the meantime Amy saw her first novel reach record sales of 2 million copies and she participated in helping to turn the novel into a successful movie. Released in 1993, *The Joy Luck Club* was directed by Wayne Wang and adapted to the screen by Amy Tan, who also received credit as one of the film's producers. In addition, she appears briefly in the movie's first party scene.

After failing to bring *The Year of No Flood* to press because she believed she discussed it too much, Tan published her third adult book, *The Hundred Secret Senses*, in 1995, with practically no advance comment. Rather than explore the mother/daughter bond that was so prevalent in her previous two novels, Amy chose to explore the strained relationship between two half-sisters, 30-year-old Olivia Yee Bishop, who is a commercial photographer, and Kwan Li, who is 12 years older than Olivia. Eccentric and spontaneous, Kwan comes to live with her Chinese-American family when in her late teens, and has often embarrassed and annoyed her younger half-sister. However, despite Olivia's attitude, throughout the years Kwan remains steadfastly devoted to Olivia. Also interwoven in the story is Kwan's belief in the supernatural and her tales

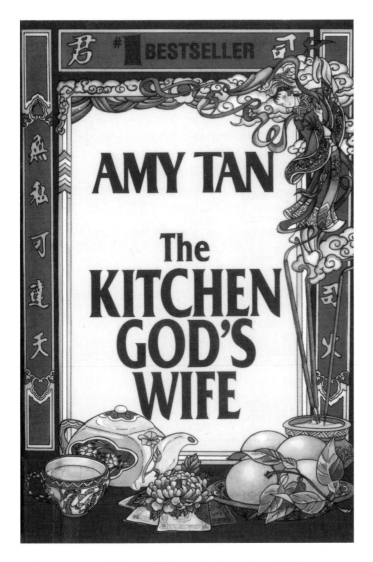

The Kitchen God's Wife, *Amy's second book, enabled her to probe aspects of her mother's life she had never understood before.*

of a previous life in China during the 1860s.

A writer for the *New York Times* summarized the essence of the new work, and its characters Olivia and Kwan, this way: "The novel is about how the experiences of the past visit the present with a vengeance and how easy it is to misunderstand people, even family, when you don't know all they have been through. The novel is, Ms. Tan said, a kind of coming out for her, because it all but concludes that the supernatural is real.

If Olivia represents Ms. Tan's rational, Western side, then Kwan, who communes with spirits from the past, represents her dreamier, Eastern side, the side that believes in the unbelievable."

Several critics said they had difficulty putting aside their skepticism about ghosts and the supernatural—the ghost, or "yin," world in the novel—in order to appreciate *The Hundred Secret Senses*. Tan herself, according to an article in the *Detroit News*, has described several incidents in which she believes she has communicated with ghosts.

"I'm educated, I'm reasonably sane," Tan told *Salon* magazine, "and I know that this subject is fodder for ridicule. To write the book, I had to put that aside. As with any book, I go through the anxiety, 'What will people think of me for writing something like this?' But ultimately, I have to write what I have to write about, including the question of life continuing beyond our ordinary senses." The response to this book was mixed, however, as a number of reviewers faulted Tan for asking readers to accept reincarnation and a hidden world of a spirits.

In 1996, shortly after the publication of *The Hundred Secret Senses*, Amy returned to China. At the invitation of a charitable foundation in Beijing, she had planned to deliver a speech to raise funds for Chinese orphans, a fitting topic for someone who had written so extensively about characters who had lost their families.

So she was surprised and dismayed, as were all guests in attendance, when Chinese police stormed the fund-raising dinner, which was taking place at a Beijing hotel. The excuse was that the organizers had failed to gain police approval for the event and the authorities forbade Tan to deliver the speech. The U.S. ambassador was present. About 450 people, including prominent members of the American business community, had purchased tickets to the affair.

"We were very disappointed because the event was

aimed at raising money to help Chinese orphans," Jim McGregor, chairman of the American Chamber of Commerce in Beijing, was quoted as saying in a *Detroit News* article about the incident. "There was no political agenda—the organization was just trying to help some orphans," said another guest.

Police agreed to let the dinner go ahead, but would allow no speeches to be given. It was thought that the disruption occurred because China had been criticized by foreign human rights groups that year for neglecting and leaving unwanted orphans to die in orphanages, a

A caregiver holds a Chinese orphan. Shortly after publication of The Hundred Senses, *Amy returned to China. Police stopped her speech, at a fundraiser for Chinese orphans, because the organizers of the benefit had not sought "police approval."*

charge that the government insisted was groundless.

During the late 1990s, Tan seemed to go into a quiet period, largely because of an unexpected confluence of personal sorrows and because she was working on another book. Her mother Daisy had been diagnosed with Alzheimer's disease. In New York, her friend and editor, Faith Sale—who had purchased *The Joy Luck* on the strength of only three stories and a belief in their author—was battling cancer.

Amy traveled back and forth between the East and West coasts, visiting both women for whom she cared so deeply. She found herself "thinking a lot about what endures and how you find people and lose them at the same time," Tan told the *Philadelphia Inquirer Sunday Magazine*. In 1999, Daisy Tan died at age 83 on November 22. Two weeks later, Faith Sale, 63, died from cancer.

During the 2001 *Philadelphia Inquirer* interview, Amy recalled a surprise that occurred when the family gathered to fill out the death certificate for Daisy. When she wrote her mother's English and Chinese names on the certificate, her older half-sisters corrected the Chinese family name. After Tan changed it, the sisters corrected her again, saying that the given name was wrong, too. It was not until then that Amy learned her mother's real Chinese name was Li Bingzi. Her sisters also informed Amy her grandmother's true name was Gu Jingmei.

Tan said she felt that her mother's spirit was present at that moment: "I could just hear this laughing in my ear, saying, 'What a stupid girl. You didn't even know that.' It just felt so strange, that I had been so involved in trying to capture the lives of both my mother and my grandmother for the past 15 years, and I still didn't know something so basic."

But stranger still, she felt energized by the experience, as if another landscape had suddenly opened to her. Although she had already placed a new manuscript in the hands of her publisher, she retrieved it and rewrote it, practically from beginning to end. "It was as though the whole essence of the book changed when they died," she said. "And I needed closure, which is why I threw myself back into writing." The completed book was *The Bonesetter's Daughter,* published in 2001.

The story begins when Ruth Young, a ghostwriter of self-help books, comes across a clipped stack of papers in the bottom of a desk drawer. Young has been caring for her ailing mother, LuLing, who is beginning to show the unmistakable signs of Alzheimer's disease. Written in Chinese by LuLing years earlier, when she first started worrying something was wrong with her memory, the papers that Ruth has found contain a narrative of LuLing's life as a girl in China. They also tell the story of the life of LuLing's mother, the daughter of the Famous Bonesetter from the village of Xian Xin— Immortal Heart—near the Mouth of the Mountain. Within the calligraphied pages Ruth finds the truth about a mother's heart, what she cannot tell her daughter, yet hopes her daughter will never forget.

Though not borrowed directly from Daisy's life— although Amy's grandmother appears in the photo on the book's slipcover—the author might have written the same dedication for this new novel as for *The Joy Luck Club*: "You asked me once what I would remember. This, and much more."

The Good Earth *by Pearl S. Buck was the first American bestseller based on Chinese characters and culture. Readers and moviegoers thrilled to the novel's depiction of Chinese life.*

8

THE ELEMENTS
OF TAN'S FICTION

"I don't see myself writing about culture and the immigrant experience. That's just part of the tapestry. What I believe my books are about is relationships and family."

—Amy Tan, from a 1995 interview with *The Detroit News*

Amy Tan was not the first American writer to portray Asians or Asian-Americans. But to understand the place of her work in American literature, it's important to first take a step back historically.

The first American writer to base a best-selling novel on Chinese culture and characters was Pearl Buck, the daughter of American missionaries who lived in China during the first part of the 20th century. Buck's *The Good Earth* won the Nobel Prize for literature in 1938. Although the book is a sympathetic portrayal of human beings at the mercy of fate, human desires, and natural forces, readers were also interested in the book's descriptions of strange practices—opium-smoking, feet-binding, and planned marriages—as well as the depiction of the male-dominated Chinese society.

After World War II, a spate of books appeared written by Japanese-Americans about their experiences in internment camps in the United States, but anti-Japanese sentiment was still so strong that few of the books received much attention. Instead, the first Chinese-American author to achieve financial success (and who served as a mentor to many other Asian-American writers) was C. Y. Lee. Lee's *Flower Drum Song* (1955) presented optimistic Asians adapting good-naturedly to the tidal wave of Western ideals that swept the Pacific hemisphere after World War II. The book was made into a smash Broadway play by the writing team of Rogers and Hammerstein, and then into a movie by 20th Century Fox.

In fact, what most post-World War II Americans knew about Asians—except ex-military personnel who had served in the Pacific and Far East during the 1940s—they gleaned from movies and TV. The characters presented were usually happy-go-lucky *Flower Drum Song*-types or figures from a shadowy world of intrigue that had an Asian flavor.

The reasons for this limited portrayal were that the genuine, historical roles played by Asian immigrants in building the first transcontinental railroad in the United States, working in West Coast gold mines and logging camps, and planting and harvesting California farmland and orchards, had limited entertainment value. But Oriental "quaintness"—what seemed like eccentricities involving dress, speech, manners, traditions, and so on—tended to go over well with audiences.

At the movies, for example, a series of popular detective novels gave rise to the on-screen characters of Fu Manchu, an evil, slow-speaking mandarin with long fingernails, and Charlie Chan, a pudgy detective who constantly quoted fortune-cookie proverbs that began, "Confucius say. . . ." Neither actor was Asian. In the film version of the play, *Teahouse of the August Moon* (1956), Marlon Brando, best known for American

Victor Sen Yung played Hop Sing on the long-running television western Bonanza. *Hop Sing was a combination houseboy, cook, and nurse. His main duty, however, seemed to be comic relief.*

tough-guy roles, played a silly Japanese interpreter trying to please U.S. servicemen in Okinawa.

On television, one of the longest-running, most popular prime-time programs of the 1960s, *Bonanza*, featured Chinese-American actor Victor Sen Yung playing a combination cook, nurse, and houseboy named Hop Sing. Yung minced into scenes wearing a pigtail, beanie, and white jacket, mainly for comic relief. When he got angry, he shouted in a torrent of Cantonese. A decade later, a non-Asian, David Carradine, played a seeker after ancient truths in *Kung Fu*. He was chosen for the part over martial artist Bruce Lee because Lee was thought to be too Chinese-looking (Lee was Chinese-American).

By the late 1970s, however, a new emphasis on authentic experiences of race, culture, and ethnicity encouraged a rise in better-quality literature about Asians and Asian-Americans, especially for young people. Jeanne Wakatsuki Huston and James D. Huston's *Farewell to Manzanar* (1973)—the true story of a spirited Japanese-American family's internment during World War II—was an instant hit with young readers. Linda Crew's novel *Children of the River* (1989) featured Sunder, who escapes Khmer Rouge rebels but has to cope with two cultures. The theme of cultures in conflict is treated again, but touchingly, in Bette Bao Lord's *In the Year of the Boar and Jackie Robinson* (1984), which dramatized her bewildering Chinese-American childhood in Brooklyn. Other novels featuring bi-cultural struggles include Gloria D. Miklowitz's *The War Between the Classes* (1985) in which Emiko (Amy) Sumoto learns the meaning of status; and Yoshiko Uchida's *A Jar of Dreams* (1981), the story of Rinko growing up in California during the Great Depression of the 1930s.

So it can be fairly said that American readers were receptive to, and prepared for serious stories with Asian-American settings, and bicultural characters trying to reconcile the past with the present, when Amy Tan's *Joy Luck Club* appeared in 1989. But Tan herself would be the first to object that her stories rely on culture and conflicts of culture alone. And in fact, to rank as superior literature, her work would have to be much deeper than that—and it is.

As Tan told an interviewer for the *Detroit News*, culture and the immigrant experience is just a part of what she writes about. The focus of her books is relationships and family. She noted, "I've had women come up to me and say they've felt the same way about their mothers, and they weren't immigrants."

For the most part, Amy Tan's works focus on the mother/daughter relationships she places at the center of her novels. Problems about adapting to different cultures provide fuel for drama, but rank second in importance to the personal conflicts. For her settings, she tends to prefer China before the Communist government came to power. Thematically, one of her favorite topics to explore is "women with a past." To move her characters through time and space, she relies heavily on flashbacks, storytelling, and mysticism. In *The Joy Luck Club,* for instance, Tan begins each chapter with a parable from long ago that is in some way a parallel to the life of the woman whose story is about to be told. This connection of the past and the present is one of Tan's favorite devices for hatching a story.

Relationships between Chinese mothers and American-born Chinese daughters are strained in Tan's novels, a pattern established in *The Joy Luck Club.* Mothers want to bring up their children according to the Chinese ways. Daughters want to live their own lives according to American ways, hating Chinese habits and traditions, sometimes to the extent of being ashamed of their origins. Amy's own childhood dilemmas as a "hyphenated American" have influenced many of her books.

Similar to the stories in *The Joy Luck Club,* Tan's second novel, *The Kitchen God's Wife,* explores mother/daughter clashes that spring from cultural values colliding, and of a daughter's growing understanding of and respect for her mother. Her third novel, *The Hundred Secret Senses,* again dramatizes relationships racked by differences between cultures, but this time the combatants are half-sisters, one from China, the other the child of an American mother and a Chinese father.

Establishing one's identity again serves as the cornerstone to *The Bonesetter's Daughter.* Archeologists have settled on the mother's village as the dig site for Peking Man, uncovered near Beijing in the 1920s and

Reviewers faulted Tan for asking readers to accept reincarnation and a hidden world of spirits in order to enjoy The Hundred Spirits.

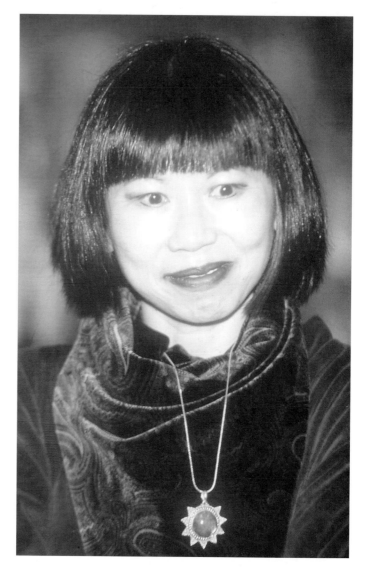

considered to illustrate the first evolutionary link between man and ape. The intriguing story of the bones' disappearance in the second world war runs congruent with Tan's perception of family history, vague, elusive, yet capable of wielding power over people. "To me, it was such a wonderful metaphor for the kind of thing that happens when you lose a parent," Tan said in the *Philadelphia Inquirer Sunday Magazine,* "that you spend a life kind of excavating who these people are and how they relate to you and the whole history of your place in the world. And then you lose them. And so much of who they were remains a mystery to you."

An element in Tan's novels that sharpens the edge of conflict between mothers and daughters is poor communication, resulting from problems with language or feelings of shame. Daughters don't know or understand their mothers because information is missing. Tan's mothers usually try to conceal a terrible secret, one that even relatives would rather ignore. In *The Joy Luck Club*, Suyuan Woo has been formerly married and lost children in China—a page taken directly from Daisy Tan's life. In *The Kitchen's God Wife*, a similar secret from the past boils beneath the surface; and in *The Hundred Secret Senses*, the father is the one who has a secret past this time—the existence of a Chinese daughter—but the mystery injects trouble into the relationship between his wife and American daughter.

Men don't usually figure very prominently in Tan's novels. One critic, Frank Chin, has accused her of altering the meaning of traditional Chinese myths involving men, and in doing so, catering to American stereotypes of Chinese men as misogynists, or women-haters. Chin argues that portraying Chinese men as insensitive and abusive undermines Asian men's struggle for racial equality. On another note regarding tradition, he also objects to Tan using the first-person or "I" voice to narrate her stories because autobiography is not a traditional Chinese form of storytelling.

Tan has said that her aim is not to provide historical information, but rather to create a work of art. Critics tend to agree, pointing out that her works are not authentically "Chinese" in nature, but are instead stories with universal themes—conflicts between generations, family members fighting for control, and so on—told by narrators searching for a balance between their Chinese heritage and American lifestyles.

Tan welcomes analysis of her work, but in a talk she often gives to students and teachers entitled, "Required Reading and Other Dangerous Subjects," she cautions against straining too hard to force meanings onto her writing. "On one occasion," she said, "I read a master's thesis on feminist writings, which included examples from *The Joy Luck Club*. The student noted I had often used the number four, something on the order of 32 or 36 times, in any case a number divisible by four." She admitted that, in fact, there were four mothers, four daughters, four sections of the book, and four stories per section.

"Furthermore," Tan continued, "there were four sides to a mah-jongg table, four directions of the wind, [and] the four players. More importantly," she postulated, "my use of the number four was a symbol for the four stages of psychological development which corresponded in uncanny ways with the four stages of some kind of Buddhist philosophy I had never heard of before."

Her point is that she finds amusing, though sometimes baffling, the lengths that readers and critics will go to find significance in her choices as an author, when her paramount goal is to tell a good story. Interpreting her images as symbols is another example, she said, of finding meaning where none was really intended.

"The truth is, I do indeed include images in my work, but I don't think of them as symbols, not in the Jungian sense [Carl Jung was a psychologist who introduced the idea that humankind uses common symbols]. . . . If there are symbols in my work, they exist largely by accident, or in someone else's interpretive design. . . . If I wrote of an orange moon rising on a dark night, I would more likely ask myself later if the image was clichéd, not whether it was the symbol of the feminine force rising in anger, as one master's thesis postulated."

Nor does she want her novels and stories to teach the

reader about China, Chinese-Americans, mothers and daughters, or Chinese cooking, for that matter. That would be propaganda, not fiction, she said. She is dismayed by literature anthologies used in schools that include her work and then provide students with end-of-the-chapter questions that serve as quizzes about "lessons" taught in the scene or story.

"One publisher wished to include an excerpt from *The Joy Luck Club*," she said, "a scene in which a woman invites her non-Chinese boyfriend to her parents' house for dinner. The boyfriend brings a bottle of wine as a gift and commits a number of social gaffes at the dinner table.

"Students were supposed to read this excerpt, then answer the following question: 'If you were invited to a Chinese family's house for dinner, should you bring a bottle of wine?'"

In Amy's novels, mothers usually conceal terrible secrets from their daughters. In The Joy Luck Club, *Suyuan Woo has concealed a previous marriage and children from her daughter.*

Amy has become known for her chic clothes and accessories–flowing capes, jade jewelry, big hats, and dark colors–and for her habit of smiling mischievously.

9

AMY TAN TODAY

"I think that if everything were neatly resolved, I would have no more stories to write."

—Amy Tan, in an interview with *The New York Times*

In a large condominium in the upscale Presidio district of San Francisco, Amy Tan and her husband Lou DeMattei occupy the entire top floor of an immense early-20th century house. Large windows frame picture-postcard views of the Golden Gate Bridge spanning the sparkling blue waters of the Pacific. Visitors to the couple's home say the inside is decorated in a kind of Chinese-American theme. Dark woods, shutters on the windows, vases filled with fresh flowers, and rich hues on the walls of red and orange create a sense of the Chinese past. Yet there are also Hollywood-type posters of Asian beauty queens from the 1940s and antique parasols, which seem to say, "Here's how America romantically imagines Chinese culture."

Tan and her husband have no children. "I remember being

such an unhappy child," she told a *New York Times* interviewer, "and I can't guarantee that I won't do the same things my mother did." However, Tan's miniature Yorkshire terriers, peeping out from the oversized handbags she carries, have become as much associated with her public image as her chic clothes and accessories—flowing capes, jade jewelry, big hats, and dark colors—and her habit of crossing her arms and smiling mischievously.

But she also admits to having a public self that's different from her private self. "I have a public persona, and what I do with it now *is* to have fun with it," she said. "I used to resent feeling that I was giving away bits and pieces of myself—that my privacy was being invaded—but now I happily give away this part of my persona which is just the fun part. I used to dread the readings, and go home and gnash my teeth, and now I just do it and it's over. I forget it and I just go back to the non-persona, the private persona, which can be fun too."

In an interview with the *New York Times,* she explained that she prefers her privacy. She can be more comfortable at home, she says, "when I'm walking around back home with my husband, or when I'm having a conversation with him, and he's sort of drifting off trying to read the paper, and I say: 'Well, this is good; I'm as boring as I always was.'"

Being in the public eye, especially when on tour promoting one of her books, can be tiring, she said. "You never want to complain," she confessed in an interview for *San Francisco Magazine,* "because the people who don't get to go on book tours are the ones who'd love to go. Anyone would imagine it's the most exciting thing in the world, and it would be if it lasted one or two days. But it goes on and on. You know, your makeup always has to be on. Your luggage gets lost. It's all the little things that unnerve all of us, that make us a little crabby, only you have to be in a good mood every day."

Now and then when Amy Tan is out shopping or running errands, an admirer will come up to her and ask, "Aren't you Amy Tan?" Rather than admit the truth, Amy just looks at the person and says, "You know, I've had other people who thought that, too." She maintains that she is not really lying; it's just her way of holding on to her privacy.

Tan explains that she's just having fun, that being famous is still an aspect of her life that's surprising to her. She has said that the strangest aspect of her celebrity is seeing her name on Cliff Notes, the study summaries of great literature. Although she is pleased to be "embalmed", as she puts it, in Cliff Notes with the likes of authors such as Shakespeare, Joyce, and Conrad, Tan points out that she is a contemporary author. "They are not. Since I'm not dead yet, I can talk back," she once said to a high school audience.

One thing that does bother her, however, about being a famous writer, who also happens to be Chinese-American, is that many people expect her to be a role model. A writer for *Salon Magazine* described Tan lighting up a cigarette "surreptitiously" on the balcony of her San Francisco home and apologizing to the interviewer: "I don't smoke in public, it's not a good image, it's not a good role model. Not that I actively set out to be one."

In fact, she finds it "laughable" and an "onerous burden" that anyone looks to her as a role model because "it's just something that's been thrust upon me."

"I'm not comfortable trying to be a role model," she said, "because I'd feel I'd have to modify my writing. I'd be self-censoring. I think that's a big danger as a writer."

Her books might be serious, but Amy admits to being much sillier in her personal life. She performs from time to time with Stephen King and other authors in a rock band called the Rock Bottom Remainders.

Second, she said that being pigeonholed as a kind of spokesperson of Chinese-American concerns runs the risk of ruining the artistry in her novels and stories.

"Someone who writes fiction is not necessarily writing a depiction of any generalized group, they're writing a very specific story," she told *Salon*. "There's also a danger in balkanizing literature, as if it should be read as sociology, or politics, or that it should answer questions like, 'What does *The Hundred Secret Senses* have to teach us about Chinese culture?' As opposed to treating it as literature—as a story, language, memory."

Being a writer and free to follow where the experience of writing takes her is a crucial part of Tan's life for a number of reasons. "I couldn't survive without writing. It's like breathing. I have to write," she told *AsianWeek*. "I go crazy when I don't write for a while. When I'm away from my writing, I can't stop writing in my head."

First, the act of writing allows her to revisit a place where she felt content in her otherwise difficult and often often unhappy childhood.

In the third grade, rather than having her skip a grade for which she might not have been ready psychologically, her teacher encouraged her to sit quietly instead and draw pictures of anything that came into her mind. "That was a wonderful period in my life," Tan recalled. "I mean, I didn't become an artist, but somebody let me do something I loved. What a luxury, to do something you love to do. I would still like to have that luxury, to be able to just sit and draw for hours and hours and hours. In a way, that's what I do as a writer. I just sit by myself, being in my own mind, not being directed at what I should be doing moment-by-moment, not having a clear plan set out by anybody and just letting imagination enter into the blank page."

In fact, Tan draws on her childhood and youth as reservoirs of feelings and impressions that bubble up like springs in her writing.

"This is what I try to do as a writer, I try to remember what those emotions were like when I was younger. They just didn't understand. They didn't know who I really was. They didn't know how much the smallest amount of recognition would have meant to me and how the smallest amount of criticism could undo me," she said, referring to the adults in her life.

She speaks of an especially unpleasant childhood incident, one in which adults stifled her curiosity and coerced her to behave; the experience left a lasting mark on her as a creative person and an independent thinker.

Having caught her reading a couple of medical books on sexual dysfunctions, her parents sent the family youth minister to counsel her at home. "He said how this would corrupt my mind and I would go insane and all this kind of stuff. We were seated in my parents' bedroom on my parents' bed. And, I have to tell you, what was so profound about that is that here this man, who I was supposed to trust, was telling me about these things and suddenly he saw that I was very sad because, at the same time, my father was in the hospital dying. So he said, 'Cheer up, it's not that bad.' And he threw me on the bed and he started to tickle me," Tan said.

Like most small girls, Tan sensed that being tickled by an adult male in a secluded place was wrong. But more important, it made her mistrust authority. "It made me disbelieve everything he had to say about books being bad for you. I was intelligent enough to make up my own mind. I not only had freedom of choice, I had freedom of expression.

"I think that, in part, also made me a writer," she continued, "a certain stubborn streak. I'm not advocating disobedience to authority in general—because that doesn't necessarily lead to anything—but knowing the difference between your own intelligence and somebody handing you a set of things you should believe."

Tan calls herself "a very strong advocate for freedom of speech, freedom of expression, and the danger of banning books. The danger is in creating the idea that somebody else is going to define the purpose of literature and confine who has access to it."

Another reason that being a writer is important to her is that writing has become therapy for working out lifelong inner conflicts that seem to surrender their power over her when told in stories.

According to a *New York Times* article, Tan used to have a reccurring dream in which she would try to use a pay phone, but the phone would take her money without making the connection. It seemed to be a metaphor for failing to communicate, or not being understood. But since she began writing fiction, the dream has changed: she makes the connection and money comes pouring out of the phone like a slot machine hitting the jackpot.

But that's not to say that the effect of longstanding problems, setbacks, and doubts have evaporated, either. And that's good for her creatively, she realizes. "I think that if everything were neatly resolved, I would have no more stories to write."

"It's not as though I came to one crisis, overcame that, and the rest of my life was smooth and perfect. Life is a continual series of bumps and crises. You think you're never going to get over a hurdle, and you get over it. . . .You can look back on what's just happened and you make sense of it and grow, or you stagnate or you go back down,

A strong opponent of censorship, Amy is seen here at a literary gala with actor Ron Silver.

but it's your period of existence. The hurdles and conflicts are really momentary. You get over them and you see what happens afterwards."

"I think that the other reason that I've become a storyteller," she told an interviewer for *The Sonoma Independent* newspaper, "is that I was raised with so many different conflicting ideas that it posed many questions for me in life, and those questions became a filter for looking at all my experiences and seeing them from different angles. That's what I think that a storyteller does, and underneath the surface of the story is a question or a perspective or a nagging little emotion, and then it grows."

CHRONOLOGY

1952   Born Amy Tan on February 19 to John and Daisy Tan in Oakland, California

1969   Graduates from Institut Monte Rosa Internationale high school in Montreaux, Switzerland; attends Linfield College in Oregon

1973   Receives her B.A. from San Jose University in California

1974   Receives her M.A. from San Jose University; marries Louis DeMattei

1976   Becomes a language development consultant to the Alameda County Association for Retarded Citizens

1981   Works as editor of a medical journal

1983   Becomes a freelance business writer

1985   Joins Squaw Valley Community of Writers

1987   Takes her Chinese immigrant mother to revisit China, where she meets two of her three half sisters; G. P. Putnam's Sons buys short story "Rules of the Game" and novel outline

1989   *The Joy Luck Club* published; remains on the *New York Times* best-seller list for nine months

1991   *The Kitchen God's Wife* published

1992   *The Moon Lady* published.

1993   *The Joy Luck Club* made into a feature film

1994   *The Chinese Siamese Cat* published

1995   *The Hundred Secret Senses* published

2001   *The Bonesetter's Daughter* published

- In 1989, *The Joy Luck Club* appeared for more than 40 weeks on *The New York Times* list. It was nominated for the National Book Award and the National Book Critics Award, and received the Commonwealth Gold Award and the Bay Area Book Reviewers Award. It was adapted into a feature film in 1994, for which Tan was a co-screenwriter with Ron Bass and a co-producer with Bass and Wayne Wang.

- *The Kitchen God's Wife*, published in 1991, was a *New York Times* best-seller.

- *The Hundred Secret Senses* in 1995 was a *New York Times* best-seller.

- *The Bonesetter's Daughter* was a *New York Times* best-seller in 2001.

- Tan's short stories and essays have appeared in *The Atlantic, Grand Street, Harper's, The New Yorker, Threepenny Review, Ski,* and others. Her essay, "Mother Tongue," was chosen for Best American Essays in 1991 and has been widely anthologized.

- She was the editor for the 1999 edition of *Best American Short Stories*.

- Tan's novels and stories have been translated into Chinese, Japanese, Korean, Spanish, German, French, Italian, Dutch, Portuguese, Catalan, Finnish, Norwegian, Swedish, Danish, Icelandic, Russian, Estonian, Serbo-Croatian, Czech, Polish, Hebrew, Greek, Tagalog, and Indonesian.

- She has also written two children's books, *The Moon Lady* (1992) and *The Chinese Siamese Cat* (1994).

FURTHER READING

Nonfiction

Berger, Laura Standley, ed., et al. *Twentieth Century Young Adult Writers*. Washington D.C.: St James Press, 1994.

Bloom, Harold, ed. *Amy Tan*. Philadelphia: Chelsea House Publishers, 2000.

Chan, Sucheng, *Asian Americans: An Interpretive History*. Boston: Twayne Publishers, 1991.

Chapman, Jeff, and John D. Jorgenson, eds. "Amy Tan." *Contemporary Authors*, Vol. 54. Detroit, Mich.: Gale Research, 1997.

Chiu, Christina. "Amy Tan" in *Lives of Notable Asian Americans*. Philadelphia: Chelsea House Publishers, 1996.

Chu E. and C.V. Schuler.*Our Family, Our Friends, Our World: An Annotated Guide to Significant Multicultural Books for Children and Teenagers*. New York: R. R. Bowker, 1992.

Graham, Judith, ed. "Amy Tan" in *Current Biography Yearbook, 1992*. New York: H. W. Wilson Company.

Hong, Maria. ed. *Growing Up Asian American*. New York: W. Morrow, 1993.

Huntley, E. D. *Amy Tan: A Critical Companion*. Westport, Conn.: 1998.

Jenkins, E. C. and M.C.Austin. *Literature for Children about Asians and Asian Americans: Analysis and Annotated Bibliography*. Westport, Conn.: Greenwood Press, 1987.

Kramer, Barbara. *Amy Tan: Author of The Joy Luck Club*. Springfield, N.J.: Enslow Publishers, Inc., 1996.

Ling, Amy. *Between Worlds: Women Writers of Chinese Ancestry*. New York: Pergamon Press, 1990.

Shawn Wong, ed. *Asian American Literature: A Brief Introduction and Anthology*. New York: HarperCollins, 1996.

Zia, Hel and Susan B.Gall, eds. "Amy Tan" in *Notable Asian Americans*. New York: Gale Research, 1995.

FURTHER READING

Fiction

Chan, Jeffrey, et al., eds. *The Big Aiiieeeee! An Anthology of Chinese American and Japanese American Literature.* New York: Meridian, 1991.

Choi, Sook Nyul. *Year of Impossible Goodbyes.* Boston: Houghton Mifflin, 1991.

Hagedorn, Jessica, ed. *Charlie Chan is Dead: An Anthology of Contemporary Asian American Fiction.* New York: Penguin, 1993.

Kingston, Maxine Hong . *The Woman Warrior.* New York: Random House, 1976.

—————————————————, *China Men.* New York: Knopf, 1980.

Lee, Gus. *China Boy.* New York: Dutton: 1991. Reprint, New York: Plume, 1994.

Tan, Amy. *The Bonesetter's Daughter.* New York, Putnam, 2001.

———. *The Chinese Siamese Cat.* New York: Maxwell Macmillan International, 1994.

———. *The Hundred Secret Senses.* New York: G. P. Putnam's Sons, 1995.

———. *The Joy Luck Club.* New York: Putnam, 1989.

———. *The Kitchen God's Wife.* New York: Putnam, 1991.

———. *The Moon Lady.* New York: Macmillan, 1992.

Yep, Laurence, ed. *American Dragons: Twenty-Five Asian American Voices.* New York: HarperCollins, 1993.

BIBLIOGRAPHY

"Amy Tan Talks with *San Francisco.*" *San Francisco Magazine* Online. March, 2001. *www.sanfran.com/features/SF0103q&a.html*

"Amy Tan." 1st Person. KRT Interactive. No date.

"Amy Tan." American Academy of Achievement. (Interview) June 28, 1996. *www.achievement.org/autodoc/page/tan0int-1*

"Amy Tan." Bedford/St. Martin's Literature Links. Copyright 1999. *www.bedfordstmartins.com/litlinks/fiction/tan.htm*

"Amy Tan: *The Bonesetter's Daughter.*" Penguin/Putnam (news release). No date. *www.penguinputnam.com/static/packages/us/amytan/start.html*

1994. *http://dolphin.upenn.edu/%7Emosaic/fall94/page15.html*

"Beijing Stops Amy Tan Speech." *The Detroit News.* April 1, 1996. *www.detnews.com/menu/stories/42195.htm*

Balée, Susan. "True to Form." (Review of *Bonesetter's Daughter*) *The Philadelphia Inquirer.* February18, 2001. *http://inq.philly.com/content/inquirer/2001/02/18/books/BONE18.htm*

Bloom, Harold, ed. *Amy Tan.* Philadelphia: Chelsea House Publishers, 2000.

Chapman, Jeff and John D. Jorgenson, eds. "Amy Tan" in *Contemporary Authors*, Volume 54. Detroit, Mich.: Gale Research. 1997.

Chiu, Christina. "Amy Tan" in *Lives of Notable Asian Americans.* Philadelphia: Chelsea House Publishers, 1996.

Carreon, Crystal. "Schools: Tan Speaks Candidly at Castilleja." *Palo Alto Weekly.* November 28, 1997. *www.service.com/PAW/morgue/news/1997_Nov_28.TAN.html*

Cujec, Carol. "Excavating Memory, Reconstructing Legacy." The World & I Online. July, 2001. *www.worldandi.com/public/2001/july/bonecut.html*

Dew, Robb Forman. "Pangs of an Abandoned Child." (Book review of *The Kitchen God's Wife*) *The New York Times.* June 16, 1991.

Feldman, Gayle. "*The Joy Luck Club*: Chinese Magic, American Blessings and a Publishing Fairy Tale." *Publishers Weekly.* July 7, 1989.

Ganahl, Jane. "Amy Tan Gets Her Voice Back." *Book: The Magazine of the Reading Life.* January/February, 2001. *www.bookmagazine.com/issue14/tan.shtml*

Gates, David and Dorothy Wang. "A Game of Show Not Tell." *Newsweek*. April 17, 1989.

Giles, Gretchen. "Ghost Writer." (Interview with Amy Tan) *The Sonoma Independent*. December 14-20, 1995. *www.metroactive.com/papers/sonoma/12.14.95/tan-9550.html*

Graham, Judith, ed. "Amy Tan" in *Current Biography Yearbook, 1992*. New York: H. W. Wilson Company.

Hayn, Judith and Deborah Sherrill. "Female Protagonists in Multicultural Young Adult Literature: Sources and Strategies." *The ALAN Review*. Fall, 1996. *http://scholar.lib.vt.edu/ejournals/ALAN/fall96/f96-09-Hayn.html*

Holt, Patricia. "Between The Lines—Students Read a Lot into Amy Tan." *San Francisco Chronicle*. August 18, 1996.

Hubbard, Kim and Maria Wilhelm. "*The Joy Luck Club* Has Brought Writer Amy Tan a Bit of Both." *People*. April 10, 1989.

Huntley, E. D. *Amy Tan: A Critical Companion*. Westport, Conn.: Greenwood Publishing Group. 1998.

Koenig, Rhoda. "Heirloom China." *New York*. March 20, 1989.

Kramer, Barbara. *Amy Tan: Author of* The Joy Luck Club. Springfield, N.J.: Enslow Publishers, Inc. 1996.

Lew, Julie. "How Stories Written for Mother Became Amy Tan's Best Seller." *The New York Times*. July 4, 1989.

Lyall, Sarah. "At Home with Amy Tan: In the Country of the Spirits." *The New York Times*. February 28, 1995.

Messud, Claire. "Ghost Story." (Review of *The Hundred Secret Senses*) *The New York Times*. October 29, 1995.

Miner, Valerie. "The Daughters' Journeys." *Nation*. April 24, 1989.

Nelyvbeld, Nita. "Mother as Muse." *Philadelphia Inquirer Sunday Magazine*. February 18, 2001.

Pin-chia Feng, "Amy Tan." *Dictionary of Literary Biography*. Vol. 173 (1996):281-9.

"An Interview with Amy Tan." *Mosaic* magazine. Fall, 1994. University of Pennsylvania.

BIBLIOGRAPHY

Rothstein, Mervyn. "A New Novel by Amy Tan, Who's Still Trying to Adapt to Success ." *The New York Times.* June 11, 1991.

Schecter, Ellen. "Children's Books; Girl Overboard." (Review of *The Moon Lady*) *The New York Times.* November 8, 1992.

Schell, Orville. "Your Mother Is in Your Bones." (Book Review of *The Joy Luck Club*) *The New York Times.* March 19, 1989.

Schleier, Curt. "The Joy Luck Lady." *The Detroit News.* November 3, 1995.

See, Carolyn. "Drowning in America, Starving in China." *Los Angeles Times.* March 12, 1989.

Tan, Amy. "Angst and the Second Novel." *Publishers Weekly.* April 5, 1991.

Tan, Amy. "Watching China." *Glamour.* September, 1989.

"The Spirit Within." *Salon Magazine* (Interview with Amy Tan). November 12, 1995. *www.salon.com/12nov1995/feature/tan.html*

"Voices from the Gaps: Women Writers of Color" (Amy Tan) University of Minnesota. December 6, 1996. *http://voices.cla.umn.edu/authors/AmyTan.html*

Walter, von Yvonne. "The 'Ayatollah of Asian America' versus the 'Woman Warrior': Remarks on the Chinese American Literary War." Twin Peaks. University of Leipzig. 1997. *www.uni-leipzig.de/~amerika/tp/tp_309.htm*

INDEX

INDEX

PICTURE CREDITS

Charles J. Shields writes from his home near Chicago, Illinois, where he lives with his wife, Guadalupe, an elementary school principal. Shields was chairman of the English Department at Homewood-Flossmoor High School in Flossmoor, Illinois. This is his third book for Chelsea House Publishers.

Matina S. Horner was president of Radcliffe College and associate professor of psychology and social relations at Harvard University. She is best known for her studies of women's motivation, achievement, and personality development. Dr. Horner has served on several national boards and advisory councils, including those of the National Science Foundation, Time Inc., and the Women's Research and Education Institute. She earned her B.A. from Bryn Mawr College and her Ph.D. from the University of Michigan, and holds honorary degrees from many colleges and universities, including Mount Holyoke, Smith, Tufts, and the University of Pennsylvania.